Dr. Jason Allen has written a needed book that will bless, encourage, and instruct pastors, seminarians, and everyday disciples. *Being a Christian* is easy-to-read and biblically sound, explaining what it means to experience the gospel's power in the most pressing areas of our lives, including marriage, work, and our churches. Filled with relatable examples and theological insight, new and mature believers alike will be reminded that being a Christian is never what we can do for God, but what He has done and continues to do in us through the gospel of Jesus Christ. I highly recommend it.

Thom S. Rainer, president and CEO,
LifeWay Christian Resources

One of the most pressing needs for the life of discipleship is the ability of the Christian to press the gospel, so to speak, into every corner of the room. That's what makes *Being a Christian* so incredibly helpful. It simply, insightfully, and practically helps followers of Jesus embrace the call to devote "every square inch" to their Lord and Savior.

Jared C. Wilson, director of Content
Strategy & Managing and editor of
For the Church at Midwestern Seminary

There are a lot of definitions in our culture of what it means to be a Christian. Jason Allen has written a helpful book that reminds us what Jesus has done, and how the gospel speaks into every area of our life. It is a timely reminder of what it means to follow Jesus.

Matt Carter, pastor of preaching and vision at
The Austin Stone Community Church, Austin, Texas

Anyone wanting to explore how the gospel of Jesus Christ transforms every part of life, but especially those whose spiritual roots are newly grounded in Christ, would profit by reading Dr. Allen's book, *Being a Christian*. One of its many strengths is how readable it is for people who have little familiarity with the Bible. Not all seminary presidents could write a book so accessible to the person who doesn't even know what a seminary is or does. Not all Christian writers could produce a book with such insight and integrity on how the gospel applies to the heart, the mind, the home, the workplace, the church, and more. You can read and gift this book with confidence.

Donald S. Whitney, professor of Biblical Spirituality
and associate dean at The Southern Baptist Theological
Seminary, Louisville, Kentucky; author of *Spiritual
Disciplines for the Christian Life* and *Praying the Bible*

My friend, Jason Allen, has a proven record as a happy and healthy pastor, theologian, and organizational leader. But more than that, I personally know him to be a faithful husband, father, and friend. This book offers help to any Christian who seeks to apply the gospel comprehensively to every area of life.

Jimmy Scroggins, lead pastor,
Family Church, West Palm Beach, Florida

I commend to you Jason K. Allen's new book, *Being a Christian*. This book will serve well those who have yet to make a decision to follow Christ, as well as those who have been Christ-followers for years. It deals with a plethora of subjects, most of which are struggles for the majority of us. Please listen to the solid experience, biblical scholarship, and personal passion behind these words. The heart message of this book will help you, not to follow a list of rules, but to fall in love with a God who loves you and wants you to draw near to Him in every part of your life.

Frank S. Page, PhD, president and
CEO, Executive Committee
of the Southern Baptist Convention

When Jesus enters into your life, your entire life is impacted; no area remains unaffected. This book is written by a godly and gifted leader who lives out this message in every area of his life. Read it. Share it. Live it."

Ronnie Floyd, senior pastor, Cross Church;
president, National Day of Prayer;
former president, Southern Baptist Convention

Being a Christian is one of the best short books I've read on the Christian life. Jason Allen displays his shepherd's heart as he walks us through the biblical basics of vibrant faith. The text is at once sweeping in its scope—giving us an IMAX vision of a gospel-captivated existence—while never intimidating the reader. We come away from Allen's book much the way Christ's disciples felt after spending time in his presence: invigorated, excited, humbled, and ready to seek still more glory for our Lord and Savior.

Owen Strachan, associate professor of
Christian Theology, Midwestern Baptist
Theological Seminary; author, *Risky Gospel:
Abandon Fear and Build Something Awesome*

JASON K. ALLEN

BEING A

CHRISTIAN

HOW JESUS REDEEMS ALL OF LIFE

PUBLISHING GROUP

NASHVILLE, TENNESSEE

978-1-4627-6193-7

Published by B&H Publishing Group
Nashville, Tennessee

Dewey Decimal Classification: 248.84
Subject Heading: CHRISTIAN LIFE / DISCIPLESHIP /
CHRISTIAN ETHICS

Cover design and illustration © Dave Wright,
Midwestern Baptist Theological Seminary.

1 2 3 4 5 6 7 • 22 21 20 19 18

This book is dedicated, with deep appreciation, to my parents, Ray and Sandra Allen. It is impossible to overstate the influence of one's parents, and it would be impossible for me to overstate all my parents have done for me. Mom and dad, I love you, thank God for you, and pray this book, and the ministry the Lord has entrusted to me, bring you much joy and pride.

CONTENTS

FOREWORD

Scripture says one of the main identifying marks of authentic Christianity is a fervent devotion to righteous living. Christ "gave Himself for us to redeem us from every lawless deed, and to purify for Himself a people for His own possession, *zealous for good deeds*" (Titus 2:14, emphasis mine). That's why every Christian should have a driving desire to pursue holiness with a passion.

That idea may cause some serious cognitive dissonance for the typical churchgoer today because millions of Christians have been taught that it distorts or compromises the gospel to stress the need for godly behavior, or to suggest that righteous works are the inevitable fruit of authentic faith. Lots of preachers and evangelists go out of their way to avoid mentioning God's commandments, Christ's lordship, or even the gospel's call to repentance and discipleship. It is a common misconception among people who sit under such teaching that good works are incompatible with, perhaps even hostile to, divine grace. Thus any plea for virtue or piety is likely to draw the charge of legalism.

As a result, I fear many churches are filled with superficial, false converts who have never really believed the gospel at all. They've heard that Jesus promised abundant life, but they have never actually entered into that life. Many people give lip service to Christianity as the religion they want to identify with, but comparatively few lives have truly been transformed by Christ and the gospel. Wrong ideas about the gospel abound in our generation. The low spiritual state of so many western evangelical churches is the result of all that confusion.

It is true that Romans 4:5 says, "To the one who *does not work,* but believes in Him who justifies the ungodly, his faith is credited as righteousness" (emphasis mine). And of course one of the most famous gospel texts in all of Scripture is Ephesians 2:8–9: "By grace you have been saved through faith; and that not of yourselves, it is the gift of God; *not as a result of works,* so that no one may boast" (emphasis mine). We affirm the vital principle of *sola fide* ("faith alone")—that faith is the sole instrument of justification. This means from that first moment when a repentant sinner "turns to God from idols to serve a living and true God" (1 Thess. 1:9), that person is fully justified—covered with the righteousness of Christ; given a right standing with God, together with the full privileges of adult sonship; "rescued . . . from the domain of darkness, and transferred . . . to the kingdom of [God's] beloved Son" (Col. 1:13).

All of that pertains to *justification*. But the full scope of God's saving work also includes *sanctification*—growth in holiness and good works. Immediately after the biblical text says we are saved "not as a result of works," the very next verse says, "We are His workmanship, created in Christ Jesus *for good works,* which God prepared beforehand so that we would walk in them" (Eph. 2:10, emphasis mine). "If anyone is in Christ, he is a new creature; the old things passed away; behold, new things have come" (2 Cor. 5:17). Indeed, the principle of grace itself "instruct[s] us to deny ungodliness and worldly desires and to live sensibly, righteously and godly" (Titus 2:12).

The redeemed are part of a God-ordained long-range plan. The Bible says believers are chosen and effectually drawn to Christ by God himself, who has a very specific goal in mind. In the apostle Paul's words, we are "called according to His purpose" (Rom. 8:28). And what is that purpose? "To become conformed to the image of His Son" (v. 29). God is gradually maturing us so that we are becoming more and more like Christ. The apostle John stressed that same truth: "Beloved, now we are children of God, and it has not appeared as yet what we will be. We know that when He appears, we will be like Him" (1 John 3:2).

A Christian who is not experiencing growth in grace is a living contradiction. All of us still struggle with sin and temptation, and we sometimes fail—even egregiously. But when someone exhibits no growth whatsoever, has no real love for Christ, and thinks nothing of sin, that person has no reason to imagine he or she is a genuine believer. The Christian life is more than a notional assent to a subset of gospel truths. True saving faith embraces all that Christ is and all that He loves. Every genuine Christian knows that He is Lord, and we are His bondservants. We desire to be holy, as He is holy. We long to share His glory. We behold that glory as we see Him the way He is revealed to us in Scripture. Furthermore, the apostle Paul says, as we gaze on that glory, we "are being transformed into the same image from glory to glory" (2 Cor. 3:18).

This, I am convinced, is the most thrilling aspect of life as a Christian. It's what the Christian life is all about—namely, that God Himself is perfecting us, and in the process, we are becoming more and more like Christ. It's an exhilarating, invigorating reality, and one of the great privileges God's grace affords those who believe. It is the quintessence of what Jesus was promising when He said, "I came that they may have life, and have it abundantly" (John 10:10).

All these truths are essential facets of the gospel message. The gospel doesn't stop with justification by faith and the principle of *sola fide* (as wonderful and essential as those truths are). We haven't truly grasped the gospel in its fullness until our hearts long to follow Christ and be like Him.

I've been preaching and writing about these themes for more than forty-five years. It's a subject that would probably be impossible to exhaust, even if the world's greatest writers were given an endless supply of paper and ink and a time frame that covered all of human history. So I'm glad that Jason Allen has undertaken to add his voice and his considerable communication skills to the effort.

This book is an excellent exposition of the gospel in an easily manageable and remarkably clear presentation, suitable for any reader at any stage of spiritual growth. It is insightful, thought-provoking, and heart-stirring. It communicates effortlessly some of the difficult truths that most of us have to labor hard to make clear. It is thoroughly biblical and wonderfully engaging.

I am certain you will be challenged as I was to apply your heart to greater understanding, deeper devotion, and more lively faith. I trust that as you read, God will fill you with all joy and peace in believing. May you abound in hope by the power of the Holy Spirit, and may you grow in grace and Christlikeness.

John MacArthur

INTRODUCTION

Being a Christian: How Jesus Redeems All of Life

H ave you ever renovated a house? If you have, you know the process often requires much more than you initially thought. This happened to me just a few years ago, and through that experience, I discovered a gospel analogy.

The Midwestern Seminary president's home is a beautiful structure and a special place for me and my family to live. Called the Vivion House, it's named after the original owner, Major Harvey Jackson Vivion, a Confederate officer. The major, and his descendants, occupied the house for nearly a century.

In 1957, when Southern Baptists founded Midwestern Seminary in Kansas City, the Board of Trustees purchased the bulk of the Vivion family's farmland for the upstart institution's campus. Subsequently, the Vivion family bequeathed their home and the remaining acreage to the seminary in 1966.

My family and I took up residence in the Vivion House shortly after God called us to serve Midwestern Seminary in 2012. The Vivion House has since become the Allen home—the place of a thousand family memories. But it is more than our home; it is the seminary president's home, annually hosting numerous seminary students, events, and guests.

Originally built in the 1870s, it burned to the ground in the 1940s and was rebuilt in its entirety. The sprawling, nearly ten thousand-square-foot house spans four floors.

I remember vividly the first time my family and I toured the Vivion House. Our five young children became explorers, scouring the house, rummaging through closets, and playing an impromptu game of hide-and-seek.

While my children rummaged about, my wife and I were struck by how old-worldish the house felt. You could tell it was built in another era, one for a people and a way of life foreign to our own.

We found two sets of stairs on each floor—one in the front, for the owners and guests to use, and one in the back for the attendants. The first floor featured the butler's bedroom, and the maids' apartment is still situated over the garage. Hand-crank windows and an old elevator—collapsible, sliding brass-door and all— added to the charm.

Topping things off was a servants' bell board. The set up looked like something out of *Downton Abbey*. Most every room in the house featured a call button, which the owners would press when they needed assistance. The bell board was situated over the doorway in the kitchen. The rectangular panel featured little squares, denoting each room in the house. When the owner pressed a button, the corresponding square would illumine, buzz, and vibrate.

Complementing the house are the spacious grounds, including seven barns, stables and outbuildings, two functioning wells, a gazebo, and an underground storm cellar.

After we toured the house, we were even more eager to move in, easily imagining life within it. But first, the house needed a little work—or so we thought. We anticipated a few cosmetic updates: new carpet, paint, and wallpaper. But we soon discovered that this was only the beginning.

More than Cosmetic

Once the work began, we encountered a near-daily surprise. The restorative work far surpassed all initial estimates. The main sewer line had collapsed, requiring major plumbing and concrete work in the basement. Portions of the roof had leaked for years causing significant rotting on the home's north side. The beautiful fireplaces and chimneys needed structural support. The plumbing system was a mess, the electrical system in want, insulation almost nonexistent, and the heating and cooling systems were from a previous era as well. The list of needs and the growing expenses seemed as though they would never end.

The renovation proved far more extensive, and far more necessary, than we ever imagined. Yet, when the transformation was complete, the house was far more rewarding and far more beautiful than we ever dreamed. On the backside of the transformation stood a home that was both charming and functional, ready to meet the needs of my family and the seminary I was called to serve.

A Gospel Analogy

As I reflect on the Vivion House renovation, I see a gospel analogy—an analogy that has proven true in my life, and will in yours. I see an analogy that reminds me of the scale of spiritual transformation God works in our lives, and the comprehensive way Christ changes us.

When I came to Christ as an eighteen-year-old college student, I expected something of a change, but what I had in mind was more like behavior modification than spiritual transformation. I knew Jesus died to redeem me but didn't quite understand he'd died to redeem *all of me.*

I anticipated a cleaner vocabulary, a better attitude, and a generally more moral life. In other words, I anticipated cosmetic changes: new carpet and a fresh coat of paint. But God intended—and is accomplishing—so much more. He chiseled up the foundation, knocked out walls, and rebuilt me from the inside out. He did not settle for a new paint job. He razed and rebuilt my life.

My old life was driven by self. My ambitions were selfish. My wants were selfish. My choices were selfish. I was selfish. Christ inverted all of that. My ambitions, passions, lifestyle choices, convictions became—and are becoming—shaped by Christ. His wants became my wants. His passion became my passion. He transformed me—and is transforming me—from the inside out. Jesus has redeemed all of me.

A Biblical Pattern

This is the biblical pattern. The Bible teaches us that when we come to Christ, our lives change. And it is a glorious change, one for our benefit—both for now and for all eternity.

The apostle Paul wrote extensively about his gospel transformation. In 2 Corinthians he reflected, "Therefore, if anyone is in Christ, he is a new creation;

the old has passed away, and see, the new has come!" (2 Cor. 5:17). Again, in Galatians, he wrote, "I have been crucified with Christ, and I no longer live, but Christ lives in me. The life I now live in the body, I live by faith in the Son of God, who loved me and gave himself for me" (Gal. 2:20).

This is the Christian life—Christ living his life through us.

More than Must-Do and How-To

Perhaps you are reading this book as an inquirer, considering the claims of Christ and contemplating following him. Or maybe you have experienced the grace of God through conversion but are having trouble believing it. Maybe you feel like the man in Mark 9 who declared, "I do believe; help my unbelief!" (v. 24). Then again, maybe you are genuinely following Christ but find yourself having difficulty getting traction. You seem to take one step forward only to take two steps backward. You feel defeated and are doubting God's promises. If any of these are the case, this book is for you.

This book explores the beauty of the gospel of Jesus Christ, how it impacts our lives, and what it means to follow him. This is not a how-to book because Christianity is not a how-to religion. It certainly isn't a must-do book, because Christianity isn't a must-do religion. The point of this book is not so much what you must do for Christ, but what Christ has done for you. Christianity is built upon the finished, redemptive work of Christ, and this book is about seeing, relishing, and applying his finished work.

More than a Meeting

Additionally, Christianity is more than a meeting. If you are from the Bible Belt, as I am, you may subtly think Christianity is merely about gathering with God's people. Thus, going to church is akin to following Christ and to really live the Christian life is to attend the church's activities faithfully. But the Christian life is more than keeping a few weekly appointments. Christ doesn't want to merely be included on our calendar. He wants to saturate our calendar; he wants to *be* our calendar.

If not careful, we can reduce our Christian lives to Sunday worship and an occasional Bible study or church fellowship. To do so is to minimize Christianity, practiced at appointed times with God's people. Christianity is much bigger than a couple hours a week. Christianity, as we shall see, is our life.

My aim throughout this book is to reframe your understanding of the Christian life. Prayerfully, you will discover that Christianity is not relegated to a couple "spiritual" activities a week, but you will see how the gospel invades our work, our leisure, our errands, and our families. In short, the gospel redeems and transforms all of life.

Words of Hope, Encouragement, and Promise

The message of this book is that faith in Christ has implications for every area of life. And, for us, these are words of *hope*. Every life is a story and for most of us that story includes baggage—hurtful words spoken, illicit activity enjoyed, important relationships fractured, foolish decisions made. There's not a person alive who has never needed a life mulligan. For all of this baggage, and so much more, you will see the hope of the gospel—that Jesus can change your life.

Yet, these are also words of *encouragement*. Not only can Jesus impact your life—he will. We are to be busy about pursuing him, growing in Christ, and fostering the life change he brings. In fact, at the heart of the Christian life is a paradox or, if you will, a mystery. The mystery is that although Christ is the one who changes our lives, we are responsible to pursue him and the change that he brings. The promise of the gospel invites us to rest in the grace of God but also to pursue it.

Most of all, though, these are words of *promise*. The message of Jesus, and the benefits he brings, is a promise as timeless, unchanging, and all-powerful as God himself. Thus, the gospel is a promise—a promise of a life lived for Jesus and all the joy, peace, and satisfaction it brings. In other words, the Christian life is not a grand negotiation with Christ. It is a grand accomplishment—his grand accomplishment—applied to our lives. The outworking of that will continue until we meet him.

In Conclusion

The Christian life is a journey, and your reading this book is a significant step in it.

As you read, I want you to explore with me the gospel and its implications for your life. As you do, anticipate God to work dramatically in your life. This is what he does; this is what we need.

Someone once quipped, "If your religion hasn't changed your life, you need to change your religion." Thankfully, when we embrace the gospel, such life change follows. That's because Jesus died for more than your behavior modification; he died to redeem *you* and all that entails.

You & the Gospel

Since this book is about the Christian life, and how the gospel empowers us to live it, we must begin with one massive caveat: you will not be able to live the Christian life unless you are a Christian. It is not until you are a Christian that the life of Christ is in you. The gospel is the door that leads one to life in Christ, the Christian life.

That's why, before we get too deep into this book on how the gospel redeems us, we need to pause and reflect on the most urgent of all questions: what is the gospel? What do we mean when we speak of preaching the gospel? Or sharing the gospel? Or believing the gospel? What does this word *gospel* mean?

What Is the Gospel?

In short, when we refer to "the gospel," we are refer-ring to a message about a man, Jesus Christ. The word *gospel* simply means "good news." It is the message of good news about the man Jesus Christ. This news is summarized in places like John 3:16, "For God so loved the world in this way: He gave his one and only Son, so that everyone who believes in him will not perish but have eternal life," and 2 Corinthians 5:21, "He made the one who did not know sin to be sin for us, so that in him we might become the righteousness of God."

While John 3:16, 2 Corinthians 5:21, and many other verses present the gospel in encapsulated form, the broader narrative of the gospel message runs throughout Scripture. In fact, the gospel story begins before Scripture, in eternity past, when God the Father, Son, and Holy Spirit, purposed to create all that is—a creation intended to bring them glory. And, within that creation, they chose to redeem a people to reflect their glory throughout eternity future.

In the Garden

The earliest words of Scripture both introduce and foreshadow this gospel message. In Genesis 1 and 2, we learn of a sovereign God who created all that is within the universe, including Adam and Eve. The Bible begins, "In the beginning God created the heavens and the earth." The climactic act of God's creative work came on day six, when he created man in his own image.

God not only created the first couple, he positioned them in an ideal setting—the garden of Eden. This location was perfect, facilitating a perfect life for God's perfect couple. From the garden of Eden, Adam and Eve were called to husband the land, to exercise dominion over God's broader creation, and to enjoy and glorify God forever.

As the product of a perfect and holy God, his creation was perfect and holy. It was unimprovable and a place in which Adam and Eve could enjoy perfect harmony with God and one another. Everything about Adam, Eve, the garden of Eden, and the totality of God's creative work radiated his glory.

The Original Sin

Yet Satan, appearing in the form of a serpent, persuaded Eve and, ultimately, Adam to eat of the Tree of the Knowledge of Good and Evil. The serpent was cunning, devilishly brilliant. He persuaded Adam and Eve to doubt God's Word and to believe that if they ate of the fruit, they would become like God. Cue the ominous background music and read with me Genesis 3:1–6:

Now the serpent was the most cunning of all the wild animals that the LORD God had made.

He said to the woman, "Did God really say, 'You can't eat from any tree of the garden'?" The woman said to the serpent, "We may eat the fruit from the trees in the garden. But about the fruit of the tree in the middle of the garden, God said, 'You must not eat it or touch it, or you will die.'"

"No! You will not die," the serpent said to the woman. "In fact, God knows that when you eat it your eyes will be opened and you will be like God, knowing good and evil." The woman saw that the tree was good for food and delightful to look at, and that it was desirable for obtaining wisdom. So she took some of its fruit and ate it; she also gave some to her husband, who was with her, and he ate it.

Their sin was ruinous. It severed their relationship with God, caused their immediate spiritual death, set in motion their physical death, and plunged all of humanity into sin and death with them. In the words of the apostle Paul, "Therefore, just as sin entered the world through one man, and death through sin, in this way death spread to all people, because all sinned" (Rom. 5:12). To this day, we are now all sons and daughters of Adam.

It is impossible to understand the world we now live in without a healthy doctrine of original sin. The brokenness, poverty, illness, warfare, sexual abuse, and every other human vice trace their roots back to that ill-fated day in the garden of Eden. The emptiness our lives are marked by apart from Christ is a direct result of Adam's sin.

The Second Adam

Thankfully, the story doesn't end with Adam. All that Adam lost, the second Adam—Jesus Christ—gained on our behalf. And that is precisely what all of creation needed—a second Adam, a Messiah who could make right all that Adam made wrong.

Throughout the Old Testament, the prophets foretold of one who would come and deliver God's people from their sins. The sacrificial system depicted the coming sacrifice, Jesus, who would die for our sins. Every time a priest sacrificed a spotless lamb, it foreshadowed, "The Lamb of God, who takes away the sin of the world!" (John 1:29).

Thus, when Jesus came on the scene, he arrived in a season of pent-up messianic expectation. The Jews' desire for a spiritual deliverer had morphed into a desire for deliverance from Roman oppression, a deliverance from political bondage. He came to his own, but his own did not receive him.

Spiritual Deliverance

But that wasn't Jesus' mission. His task wasn't to deliver his countrymen from political bondage. It was to save sinners from their spiritual bondage. Born of a virgin, Jesus was fully God and fully man. He lived a sinless life, performed countless miracles, and throughout his earthly ministry demonstrated he was God's only Son. As Peter declared in Matthew 16:16, he indeed was the Christ, the Son of the living God.

Not only did Jesus' disciples recognize his claim to deity, so did his detractors. In fact, throughout the New Testament, we see the Jewish leaders seeking to stone Jesus, precisely because he claimed to be God's Son, making himself equal with God.

So, Jesus, as the spotless Lamb of God, died for our sins—paying a sin debt we could never pay. In so doing, he purchased us from the slave block of sin, redeeming us for his own. And on the third day, Jesus rose from the dead.

Jesus' resurrection demonstrated that he was God's divine Son and that the Father accepted his payment for our sin. Now, Jesus is seated at the right hand of God the Father, presiding over the cosmos, interceding for his followers, and preparing to return for his people and the final judgment.

Not Just a Message, a Man

In light of this, it is essential that we remember that the gospel is not just a message; it is a man—Jesus Christ. The message is only as powerful as the Man of whom it speaks. Thus, our response is not so much a response to a message about Christ; it is a response to Christ.

We come to know Jesus and we experience his life through repentance and faith. These are gifts from God, and when we repent—turn from our sins—and place our faith in Christ, we are made right with him. This glorious transaction is summarized in Romans 5:6–9:

> For while we were still helpless, at the right time, Christ died for the ungodly. For rarely will someone die for a just person—though for a good person perhaps someone might even dare to die. But God proves his own love for us in that while we were still sinners, Christ died for us. How much more then, since we have now been declared righteous by his blood, we will be saved through him from wrath.

Saved, in Every Dimension

Through the power of Christ, the gospel saves us from our sins—in every dimension. We most often think of salvation as freeing us from the penalty of sin, and that it does. Despite conventional wisdom, there is a hell to shun and a heaven to gain. Hell is a real place, populated with real people, experiencing real, eternal punishment. And those who die apart from Christ spend eternity there. As the above passage teaches us, those who die in Christ are "saved through him from wrath." The gospel saves us from the *penalty of sin*.

The gospel also saves us from the *practice of sin*. Christians don't become perfect, but we do make progress along the way. Before our conversion, we lived, in the words of Ephesians 2:3, according to "our fleshly desires, carrying out the inclinations of our flesh and thoughts, and we were by nature children under wrath." After conversion, the Holy Spirit resides within us, enabling us to live the Christian life. Our desires change as we mature in him, and we find ourselves able to increasingly honor him with our lives.

Finally, the gospel saves us from the *pain of sin*. Many of us, perhaps you personally, live with a sense of guilt hanging over us. Filled with regret over past actions, words, or events, we wonder if God can even forgive us. As we'll see in chapter 2, the gospel makes all things new—including our past.

The Gospel for All; the Gospel for You

Remember, the gospel is for all, and the gospel is for you. There is no one beyond the reach of the gospel.

There is no one too bad to be saved; there is no one too good to need to be saved. So, as we proceed with this book, let's be clear about the gospel and its impact on one's life. Throughout this book, I'm assuming you're a believer and am orienting the book toward believers wanting to grow in Christ. But I shouldn't assume too much, and neither should you. Before you read further, reflect on the gospel, your life, and the message of Christ, and make sure you know him.

The Gospel & Your Past

O ver the years, I have had the privilege of marrying dozens of couples. When two Christians come together as one, it is always a special, joyous occasion. To ensure the couple is ready for marriage, and to strengthen their forthcoming life together, I always insist upon premarital counseling. This is nonnegotiable. The couple must complete premarital counseling before I will marry them.

When visiting one-on-one with the man, there's one question I am often asked: "How much of my past should I tell her? Should I tell her about past relationships? About stupid decisions I made? About all the baggage I am carrying?"

When they ask me this question, I usually see fear in their eyes; I can hear it in their voices. They are afraid if they "come clean," their fiancé will break off the wedding, wanting to marry someone with less baggage.

Many would-be followers of Christ have a similar outlook, and many Christians live with a persistent, suffocating guilt. They question whether Christ will truly forgive them for what they have done. They feel they will never measure up spiritually, thus assigned to second-class Christian status. Nothing could be further from the truth.

Every Person Has a Past

Every person has a past. I do. You do. Everyone does. By past, I mean things we have done at a previous point in our lives that cause regret and embarrassment, if not outright shame. It is that laundry list of attitudes, actions, and events you aren't proud of. And, again, it's not just you. *Everyone's* past is marked by, at least to some degree, foolish words, reckless decisions, and sinful acts. Everyone's!

Christianity does not change your past, but it does change what you do with it—and what it does to you. This is the beauty of Christianity, the splendor of a relationship with Christ. Jesus does not reluctantly accept us in spite of our past. He pursues us, calls us, loves us, and uses us, fully aware of our past—regardless of how checkered it may be.

The Apostle Paul

Did you know God can actually get greater glory when he uses people with a checkered past? That is the story of the greatest Christian who ever lived, the apostle Paul. He may well have had the worst past ever to overcome.

He wrote thirteen New Testament letters and traversed the Mediterranean region on three major missionary journeys. This mighty man of the faith planted numerous churches, won multitudes to faith in Christ, and laid the doctrinal foundation on which the church has ministered for nearly two millennia. The apostle Paul was a missionary-theologian unlike any other the world has ever known.

Before Paul, Saul

In Acts 9, Saul met the risen Christ, was gloriously converted, and was commissioned as an apostle. But before he encountered Christ in Acts 9, he appeared in Acts 7. This passage records one of the most diabolical scenes in all the Bible—the stoning of Stephen, the first martyr of the early church. In that setting, we find Saul, holding the coats of the stone throwers, rooting them on.

Then, in Acts 9, overflowing with hatred and rage, Saul goes to Damascus to persecute other or even more Christians. On that roadway, the resurrected Christ appeared to Saul, confronted him, and subsequently called Saul to himself and commissioned him into ministry.

Consider Paul's autobiographical reflection on his life before Christ, and his conversion story:

> I give thanks to Christ Jesus our Lord who has strengthened me, because he considered me faithful, appointing me to the ministry—even though I was formerly a blasphemer, a persecutor, and an arrogant man. But I received mercy because I acted out of ignorance in unbelief, and the grace of our Lord overflowed, along with the faith and love that are in Christ Jesus. This saying is trustworthy and deserving of full acceptance: "Christ Jesus came into the world to save sinners"—and I am the worst of them. But I received mercy for this reason, so that in me, the worst of them, Christ Jesus might demonstrate his extraordinary patience as an example to those who would believe in him for eternal life. (1 Tim. 1:12–16)

Did you catch that? Paul said God loved him, through Christ, so that God might get greater glory, as he doled out his grace on such a violent transgressor. Paul never got over this glorious grace. Indeed, God's grace fueled his Christian life and propelled him forward into unmatched ministry accomplishment.

Grace-Filled Accomplishment

Paul's Christian witness was so effective that he experienced constant persecution. See what his faith in Christ cost him:

> . . . far more labors, many more imprisonments, far worse beatings, many times near death. Five times I received the forty lashes minus one from the Jews. Three times I was beaten with rods. Once I received a stoning. Three times I was shipwrecked. I have spent a night and a day in the open sea. On frequent journeys, I faced dangers from rivers, dangers from robbers, dangers from my own people, dangers from Gentiles, dangers in the city, dangers in the wilderness, dangers at sea, and dangers among false brothers; toil and hardship, many sleepless nights, hunger and thirst, often without food, cold, and without clothing. Not to mention other things, there is the daily pressure on me: my concern for all the churches. (2 Cor. 11:23–28)

Paul's bold witness for Christ led to his house arrest, and ultimately his incarceration in the ancient world's most infamous jail, the Mamertine Prison. There, in an underground, cold, sewage-infested dungeon, Paul awaited his final execution. And executed he was. Church history teaches us Paul was beheaded outside of Rome in AD 67.

The New Testament letters he wrote, the churches he planted, the lives he touched, and the suffering he experienced all come together—especially given the church's unique inflection point during Paul's era—to make Paul the greatest Christian who ever lived.

Paul Overcoming His Past

What was Paul's secret to overcoming his past? Why was his past not a weight but a springboard? The key is that he looked *forward* to Christian service, not *backward* in guilt, shame, or regret.

Paul testified, "But one thing I do: Forgetting what is behind and reaching forward to what is ahead, I pursue as my goal the prize promised by God's heavenly call in Christ Jesus" (Phil. 3:13–14).

There is a difference—a massive difference—between overlooking your past and forgetting about it. Paul never overlooked his past. He wrote extensively about man's sinfulness, including his own.

The more he matured in Christ, the more self-aware he grew of his own sinfulness. In his first New Testament letter, written about AD 55, Paul referred to himself as "the least of the apostles" (1 Cor. 15:9). A few years later, in Ephesians 3:8, Paul referred to himself as "the least of all the saints." A few years later still, in

1 Timothy 1:15, Paul declared that he was "the worst of [sinners]."

Do you see the progression? The more Paul matured in Christ, the more he reflected on his life before Christ. The more theologically he thought about sin, repentance, conversion, and grace, the lower his view of himself became, and the more his view of the gospel increased.

Overcoming Your Past

In light of the apostle Paul, and Scripture's broader teaching on sin, repentance, and forgiveness, how can you best apply the gospel to your past? Reflect with me on these three steps.

View Your Sin as God Views It

The Bible gives promise-after-promise regarding forgiveness. Meditate on these verses:

- "Therefore, there is now no condemnation for those in Christ Jesus" (Rom. 8:1).
- "If we confess our sins, he is faithful and righteous to forgive us our sins and to cleanse us from all unrighteousness" (1 John 1:9).
- "Therefore, if anyone is in Christ, he is a new creation; the old has passed away, and see, the new has come!" (2 Cor. 5:17).

- "He has rescued us from the domain of darkness and transferred us into the kingdom of the Son he loves. In him we have redemption, the forgiveness of sins" (Col. 1:13–14).
- "As far as the east is from the west, so far has he removed our transgressions from us" (Ps. 103:12).

As you just saw in Psalm 103:12, God has separated your sin as far as the east is from the west; he's cast it into the sea of his forgetfulness. Remember, Jesus did not reluctantly accept Paul. On the contrary, he intentionally sought Paul and enlisted him into Christian service.

As John Stott observed, "God frees us from our bankruptcy only by paying our debts on Christ's cross. More than that. He has not only cancelled the debt, but also destroyed the document on which it was recorded."[1]

Think often upon this truth and remind yourself daily of the total forgiveness you have in Christ.

Rejoice in God's Providence

In God's perfect timing, you trusted Christ and he accepted you just as you were. In my case, I was a college athlete, having lived a relatively moral life but still in desperate need of a Savior. Yet not every past is the same. In the Bible Belt, where I am from, one's life before Christ is oftentimes more self-righteous than unrighteous. Others grow up in a more secular context, without a cultural morality insulating them from some of life's vices.

Whatever your background, whatever your past, rejoice in God's plan for your life. He led you by super-intending your steps and bringing you to a point of conversion. His providence is always good, beyond improvement. Thus, he crafted your story, including your past, for his own, optimum glory. The Puritan, John Flavel, captured this precisely:

> There is not such a pleasant history for you to read in all the world as the history of your own lives, if you would sit down and record from the beginning hitherto what God has been to you, and done for you; what evidences and out-breakings of his mercy, faithfulness, and love there have been in all the conditions you have passed through.[2]

Thus, as you reflect on your past, let it be an oppor-tunity to praise God for his kind and faithful providence.

Own Your Testimony

Do not see your past as an embarrassing prologue to be buried, but as a glorious story to be leveraged for the kingdom. Remind people, as you remind yourself, that if God can save you, he can save anyone. Rejoice in the mire from which you were saved; celebrate publicly

God's goodness in your life. As you do, you'll encourage others and embolden yourself.

Philip Holmes stated this well when he wrote, "The gospel is so powerful that it doesn't have to undo our past sins. Instead, it redeems them and turns them around for our good and for God's glory."[3]

In Conclusion, Grace Really Is Amazing

If the apostle Paul is the greatest Christian who ever lived, "Amazing Grace" might be the greatest hymn ever written. "Amazing Grace" is to the hymn book what Psalm 23 is to the Bible—a classic text known by most all people, believers and unbelievers alike.

Yet, in order to understand "Amazing Grace," you have to understand John Newton, the man who penned it. Newton was a violent man, notorious for his exploits in the slave trade.

The epitaph adorning his tombstone, drafted by Newton himself, reflected, "John Newton, Clerk, once an infidel and libertine, a servant of slaves in West Africa, was, by the rich mercy of our Lord Jesus Christ, preserved, restored, pardoned, and appointed to preach the faith he had long labored to destroy."[4]

Newton's most lasting achievement is this iconic hymn. Sung millions of times annually, "Amazing Grace" is one of the most widely sung songs in the history of the world. When reflecting upon your sinful

past and struggling with overcoming it, let these words
sink in:

Amazing grace, how sweet the sound,
That saved a wretch like me.
I once was lost but now I'm found,
Was blind, but now I see.

The Lord has promised good to me,
His word my hope secures.
He will my shield and portion be,
as long as life endures.

When we've been there ten thousand years,
Bright shining as the sun.
We've no less days to sing God's praise,
Than when we've first begun.

Friend, be encouraged. The grace Newton found,
and wrote about, is the same grace God extends to all
who call upon the name of his Son. This grace is trans-
formative, it is overwhelming, and it is free.

This grace overcomes your past and enables your
growth in the future. You will encounter this grace—as
fully explained and applied in the gospel—throughout
this book. In the chapters that follow, we will explore
how the gospel applies to other areas of our lives, and
the implications for us.

3

The Gospel & Your Marriage

Washington, D.C., is one of my favorite cities on the planet. Our capitol city radiates beauty, history, and consequence. From childhood, it has captured my imagination. In fact, as a boy, I persuaded my parents to sign me up for a school trip to D.C. and was devastated when the trip was cancelled. As a father, I have toured Washington with my family, painstakingly tracing our nation's history with them.

My interest in Washington drew me there in the fall of 2008, as my wife and I were invited to tour the White House and the West Wing. You may recall that late November 2008 was a tumultuous time. Just a couple weeks prior, Senator Barack Obama had been elected the 44th president of the United States. The country was amid a financial crisis, which had spilled over into a global economic meltdown.

When we arrived in Washington, we found the city especially tense. Our outgoing president, George W. Bush, had called a meeting of the G-20, the twenty largest economies in the world. With the heads of government from these countries in the District, the city was on double lockdown. Motorcades filled the streets; law enforcement officials roamed the grounds.

Karen and I were to be at the White House's southwest gate at 3 p.m. We had previously submitted paperwork and cleared a background check, so we were all set for our much-anticipated tour. At 2:45, my wife and I—dressed in our Sunday best—were waiting just a couple of blocks away, prepared to make our way to the White House grounds, when it started raining. It was not your typical rain shower—it was a massive downpour. We waited as long as we could, but as the clock approached 3:00, we had to walk.

At that moment, the downpour ceased, and we dashed toward our check-in point. As we walked, we encountered what appeared to be a mob. Before we saw them, we heard them. Later, on the evening news, I confirmed what I sensed we were caught in—a massive protest march for marriage equality. My wife and I had to bob-and-weave our way through a massive march on

Washington. Together, we were walking upstream, in the opposite direction of five thousand marchers chanting, jeering, and protesting, all for a way of life alien to our own.

In that milieu, I saw a parable of the Christian life in the twenty-first century. Those who are committed to the Bible as God's Word, and its standards for sexuality, gender, and marriage, will walk upstream, against the culture, in the twenty-first century and beyond.

Yet, our cultural moment gives Christians an opportunity, a platform on which we can honor God in our marriages and display his glory in our homes, especially when contrasted with such cultural confusion. In fact, few things represent the gospel and the glory of Christ better, and few things bring us more joy, than a good Christian marriage.

What Makes a Good Christian Marriage?

Perhaps no dimension of twenty-first-century life more needs redeeming than issues of human sexuality, gender, and marriage. Yet the gospel does just that—it affects us in the deepest depths of our self-understanding and self-fulfillment. You see, God has a divine intent for us, for our wholeness, for our marriages and sexuality. In Scripture, he provides a divine template for marriage, which leads to human flourishing and to human happiness.

Before we reflect on the essentials of a good Christian marriage, let's define what marriage is. Simply put, "Biblical marriage is the covenantal, conjugal union between one man and one woman for life."[1] The church, and the whole of Western civilization, has affirmed this basic understanding of marriage for nearly two thousand years.

I unashamedly stand as one whose conscience is bound by Holy Scripture, and whose convictions are reinforced by millennia of Western civilization, that the family is and is to be the conjugal, lifelong union of one man and one woman, and the children God would so bless them with.

You need not be a theologian or even a churchman to see this. You merely need to have eyes. Natural law, as well as divine revelation, attests to the family's indispensability, structure, and purpose, and the absolute necessity of marriage itself.

For us, the next question is, what makes a good Christian marriage? At its core, it is two good Christian people, joined together in holy matrimony. Yet, a good Christian marriage is so much more than this. Two good Christian people are essential for a strong, Christian marriage—but that is not enough.

To see how the gospel affects our marriage, we must go back to the very beginning when marriage was first instituted.

Embracing a Divine Plan

Marriage, along with government and the church, is one of three institutions ordained by God. Yet, long before God appointed governmental rulers or founded the church, he initiated marriage. We discover this in the earliest pages of Scripture, and as the culmination of God's creative act, in Genesis 2:

> Then the LORD God said, "It is not good for the man to be alone. I will make a helper corresponding to him. . . ."
> Then the LORD God made the rib he had taken from the man into a woman and brought her to the man. And the man said,
>
> > This one, at last, is bone of my bone
> > and flesh of my flesh;
> > this one will be called "woman,"
> > for she was taken from man.
>
> This is why a man leaves his father and mother and bonds with his wife, and they become one flesh. Both the man and his wife were naked, yet felt no shame. (Gen. 2:18, 22–25)

Note what we see in this passage. God's divine plan includes:

- *Completion:* God saw man's loneliness, knew it was not good, and created "a helper corresponding to him." The Bible teaches us that, on occasion, God sets apart individuals for a lifetime of singleness, but that is the exception, not the norm. For most of us, we experience a relational emptiness only satisfied through the spouse God gives us.

- *Compassion:* Created from himself, Adam saw in Eve "bone of my bone, flesh of my flesh." In marriage, the two become one, because the two once were one. Thus, matrimony is to be marked by a sweet communion, a relationship of love, care, and compassion.

- *Commitment:* So attracted are we to our spouse that, in the covenant of marriage, "a man leaves his father and mother and bonds with his wife." This commitment is a permanent one, wherein we say "no" to all others for all time when we say "yes" to the chosen mate God has given us.

- *Closeness:* Within the covenant of marriage, the man and woman know a closeness, an exhilaration of love that can never be known outside of marriage. As they "become one flesh," they can be "naked, yet [feel] no shame" because they are abiding in God's divine plan, a union sanctioned by him.

A Divine Plan, Reaffirmed by Christ

Mistakenly, some people view Genesis 2 as outdated, arguing Jesus was less rigid on marriage, simply promoting an ethic of love. But did you know that Jesus reaffirmed Genesis 2, indicating the permanent, unchanging nature of marriage?

Consider this exchange between Jesus and his accusers, the Pharisees:

> Some Pharisees approached [Jesus] to test him. They asked, "Is it lawful for a man to divorce his wife on any grounds?" "Haven't you read," he replied, "that he who created them in the beginning made them male and female," and he also said, "For this reason a man will leave his father and mother and be joined to his wife, and the two will become one flesh? So they are no longer two, but one flesh. Therefore, what God has joined together, let no one separate." (Matt. 19:3–6)

The pattern we see espoused in Genesis 2, affirmed throughout Scripture, and reissued by Christ himself, is a clear one. Though in Scripture we often see marriage compromised, we nonetheless see a consistent template affirmed by God. No place is this template more clearly seen than in Ephesians 5:22–33, wherein Paul explains the roles of the husband and the wife, and the picture the marriage conveys.

Celebrating a Divine Pattern

In observing other marriages, and—if I am honest, in my own marriage—when friction occurs, it is typically because either the husband or wife is drifting from God's design for them. As a rule, the more one departs from God's standard, the more severe the conflict will be.

Space does not permit a full exposition of this passage (indeed, many books have been written on this one passage), but I do want you to read it carefully, reflect on God's instructions for husband and wife, and allow me to tease out just a couple words of application. Consider Ephesians 5:22–33:

> Wives, submit to your husbands, as to the Lord, because the husband is the head of the wife as Christ is the head of the church. He is the Savior of the body. Now as the church submits to Christ, so also wives are to submit to their husbands in everything.
>
> Husbands, love your wives, just as Christ loved the church and gave himself for her to make her holy, cleansing her with the washing of water by the word. He did this to present the church to himself in splendor, without spot

or wrinkle or anything like that, but holy and blameless. In the same way, husbands are to love their wives as their own bodies. He who loves his wife loves himself. For no one ever hates his own flesh but provides and cares for it, just as Christ does for the church, since we are members of his body. For this reason a man will leave his father and mother and be joined to his wife, and the two will become one flesh. This mystery is profound, but I am talking about Christ and the church. To sum up, each one of you is to love his wife as himself, and the wife is to respect her husband.

Broadly, note key themes from this passage:

Submission: The wife is called to lovingly submit to her husband, as he submits to Christ. The pattern is to be one of gracious headship, of the husband leading his wife and family as he follows Christ. Deviating from this pattern, either through the wife's rebellion or the husband's passivity or heavy-handedness, hinders the marriage.

Sacrifice: The husband is to give himself sacrificially for his wife. The model for such sacrifice is the greatest sacrificial act of all: Jesus' death for the church. Such sacrificial love makes the wife's gracious submission to her husband not only possible, but desirable.

Sanctification: Note also, the husband is called to further his wife's own sanctification. The marital union fosters Christian growth of both the husband and the wife. Within marriage, we learn to die to our self and to put the needs of others first. Additionally, the marital union provides a healthy, holy context for our sexuality to be expressed, enjoyed, and celebrated—a sanctifying step in and of itself. As we grow in Christ, we grow in our love for one another, and vice versa.

Servant-leadership: Lastly, men, as we lead our wives, we do so with the heart of a servant-leader. There is no room for bravado or lording our spousal role. Rather, we are to be the type of servant-leader every woman longs to follow. Putting our wife's interests, and, most of all, Christ's interests, first.

Displaying a Divine Picture

Did you notice how Paul connected marriage and the church? At first glance, you may be asking, "What does my marriage have to do with the gospel and the church?" The answer is: *everything.* A healthy marriage is a picture of the gospel. Men, our love for our wives depicts Christ's love for his church. Ladies, your submission to your husband depicts Christ's headship over his church.

Every Christian marriage is a miniature lighthouse, shining the power of the gospel, the message of grace, repentance, and forgiveness. Even for unbelievers, through common grace, God's standard for marriage is applicable and beneficial. It leads to optimum marital happiness and human flourishing, but it can only be truly lived out through the power of the gospel.

In Conclusion, What Now?

I promised in the introduction that this book is not a book of must-do's and how-to's. Yet, I know this chapter has felt like that at times. That is because God is particular about marriage, giving us specific instructions and revealing to us his specific intent. Many find themselves, having previously divorced, in a challenging marriage now, or still waiting on God's person for them. Let me offer you a few final words of encouragement.

Reflect on the key passages we considered in this chapter. Remember, God has a divine plan and pattern for your marriage, and a divine picture he wants to convey. This is all for your good, for the health and prosperity of your family, and for his glory. Like every other area of your life, you cannot improve upon God's best. It is perfect—beyond improvement. Do not crash into the wave; ride it.

Be ready to repent and forgive. Marriage is a constant cycle of repentance and forgiveness. This reality struck me recently. I was conversing with a young man about his marriage, and in the conversation he mentioned their marriage seemed like a cycle of repentance and forgiveness. I encouraged him by confirming that is *exactly* what a good marriage is. A healthy marriage is not the absence of sin; it is the presence of repentance, forgiveness, and grace. A bad marriage is one where sin is present, but repentance and forgiveness are not.

If you are single and longing for marriage, wait on the Lord. Trust that if it is his will, he will bring you a spouse who meets the biblical criteria, is a growing Christian, and who embraces these passages we have considered together. Marriage is too important, and your future too precious, to become unequally yoked with an unbeliever.

Consider anew the goodness of the gospel. Only through the gospel can you and your spouse enjoy a flourishing marriage. Yet, through the gospel, you can have just that. Settle for nothing less, and realize that as you do, your marriage will be a potent gospel witness, a little lighthouse for Christ for all who know you.

The Gospel &
Your Family

I n all of sports, there is no event quite like game
seven of Major League Baseball's World Series.
As residents of Kansas City, my family and I have
more than enjoyed following the Royals and their World
Series runs in 2014 and 2015. While the Royals were
crowned the 2015 World Series champions, it was the
2014 World Series that taught me a gospel and family
lesson.

You may recall the setting. All tied up at three
games apiece, the Royals hosted the San Francisco
Giants for the determinative game seven. My wife and I
scored tickets to the much-anticipated finale and looked
forward to rooting our team on to victory.

In the bottom of the ninth, with two outs, Kansas City trailed 3–2, when Royals left fielder, Alex Gordon, roped one to left-center field. It looked to be a single, but in an unbelievable turn of events, the Giants left fielder bobbled the ball. Gordon rounded first, picked up speed into second, and barreled toward third. For a few moments, it looked as though the impossible might happen—Gordon might have an inside-the-park homerun.

Kauffman Stadium exploded. Pandemonium pulsated through the crowd. Every Royals fan in the stadium kept yelling, "Home! Go home! Home!" More than forty thousand fans had the same thought: send him home.

The Stakes Are High

I have reflected on that final scene countless times and always see within it a life metaphor. We all know people, often men, who seem reluctant to go home. Fiddling after hours at work, taking unnecessary business trips, indulging in excessive hobbies or other such distractions that keep them from their families. We look at them and think to ourselves: *go home.* Be with your family. Love them, serve them, lead them. Go home.

Do not forget, when it comes to the family, the stakes are high. Divorce, cohabitation, out-of-wedlock children, the redefinition of marriage, and the general breakdown of the family all present a massive challenge to society—and the church. In fact, the statistics are alarming.

Consider:

- It is well documented that about 50 percent of marriages will end in divorce.[1]
- In the United States, a divorce occurs every thirty-six seconds.[2] That is roughly 2,400 divorces a day, 16,800 divorces a week, and 876,000 divorces a year.[3]
- Regarding cohabitation, Barna has reported that 65 percent of Americans believe that cohabitation is a good idea, and 57 percent of the population has at one time, or is currently, cohabitating.[4]

These statistics rightly cause us pause. If we are to respond in a way that glorifies Christ, we must first understand his design and purpose for marriage and the family.

A Divine Pattern

As we saw in the last chapter, God ordained the family. It is rooted in the created order, celebrated and supported throughout Scripture, and given by God for human flourishing—for believers and unbelievers alike. By God's common grace, even unbelievers and secular societies benefit from intact families and should be motivated to uphold and celebrate them. Thus, the family has long been recognized as the singular indispensable unit of every healthy society.

We can define a family as "the covenantal union of a man and woman for life, and the children with which God blesses them." This definition focuses on the nuclear family—parents and their children, whether biological or adopted. The family, and how it should function, is referenced throughout Scripture; but for the sake of simplicity and as a starting point, let's return to Ephesians and consider this passage in light of our children.

> Children, obey your parents in the Lord, because this is right. Honor your father and mother, which is the first commandment with a promise, so that it may go well with you and that you may have a long life in the land. Fathers, don't stir up anger in your children, but bring them up in the training and instruction of the Lord. (Eph. 6:1–4)

Note several observations about this passage. *First, the Lord charges the father with ultimate responsibility,* including the command to rear children in the fear and admonition of the Lord. This is not a call for the mother to step down; it is a call for the father to step up.

Second, notice children are called to obey and honor their parents. This is more than a parental expectation; this is a divine imperative. To "obey" refers to their actions—their outward behavior. It means to listen attentively and to respond. To "honor" refers to their attitude; what they think and feel on the inside. To obey and to honor is like a combination lock with two digits; both are expected by the Lord and are to be cultivated by the parents.

Third, did you see the link between discipline and the instruction of the Lord? The objective of our discipline is to instill within our children the fear and teachings of the Lord. It is as though every home is a miniature church; the father and mother are to shepherd the children in the fear and admonition of the Lord, and ultimately a relationship with Christ.

Redemption, a Trickle-Down Effect

The overarching point of these verses, and the preceding ones in Ephesians 5 on the husband and wife, is that the gospel impacts our most essential human relationships, the way we interact with one another, and the type of family we seek to build. Ephesians 5:22–6:4 is an instruction manual showing us how to have a happy, Christ-honoring home. And it is important we heed its teaching.

Over the years, I have tried to assemble a few items without using the instructions. I end up with leftover parts, unassembled pieces, and an item that turns out not as I envisioned or as the instruction manual pictured.

Similarly, when a family, even a Christian family, does not follow God's template—encapsulated here in Ephesians, but taught and affirmed throughout Scripture—we set ourselves up for failure and embark on a course which limits God's glory and our happiness.

Yet, the converse is also true. For parents, our redemption has a trickle-down effect. As we follow the Lord in our own lives, we flavor our household with the grace of Christ. We rear our children in a context of God's goodness, wherein they learn through observation and experience what it means to follow Jesus. The stakes are high but so is our calling, and our opportunity, as parents.

A Redeemed Family, a Prism for God's Glory

Moreover, a redeemed family is a powerful gospel witness. This is always true, but especially so in our culture. In our society, as the family continues its downward spiral, the cheerful, intact Christian family is a little lighthouse, shining forth a different, better way. In fact, I am convinced that demonstrating healthy, happy families is one of the greatest tools the church has to influence the world.

In addition to following the teaching of Ephesians 5:22–6:4, how should a Christian family live? How does a healthy home function? What are the practical steps a Christian couple can take to honor Christ in their home and truly be a prism for God's glory? How does the gospel redeem your family? Let's think this through together.

Celebrate the Gift of Children

Remember, the Bible teaches us that, "Sons are indeed a heritage from the LORD, offspring, a reward. Like arrows in the hand of a warrior are the sons born in one's youth. Happy is the man who has filled his quiver with them. They will never be put to shame when they speak with their enemies at the city gate" (Ps. 127:3–5). It is vital that couples see children not as an interruption to their career paths, as a financial burden, or a life encumbrance. View them instead as God views them—as a blessing for you and your spouse.

Guard Your Motives

Do not parent out of your own ambition, wanting your children to accomplish feats you never could. Likewise, avoid parenting out of fear, always trying to protect your child's ego from setback or failure. Finally, whatever you do, do not parent out of pride, trying to produce perfect children so onlookers will congratulate you. All three of these motives are toxic. They will poison your relationship with your children and will corrode their spiritual formation.

Share Christ with Your Children

The most important gift you can give your children is the gift of the gospel. Do not assume they have heard it at church and do not leave it to them to connect the dots from Sunday school lessons and sermons. Share the gospel with your children plainly and straightforwardly. Most especially, do not outsource your child's spiritual formation to someone else—not even your pastor. Be thankful God has given you a strong support structure through your church but own your child's spiritual formation.

Share Christ in Front of Your Children

As you do, your children can overhear the gospel in a less intimidating, more natural context. Moreover, they will sense how important the gospel is to you, that it applies to all people, and that you value the gospel and people enough to acquaint the two.

Prioritize the Lord's Day and the Body of Christ

Many parents shuttle their kids from the nursery, to the children's ministry, to the student ministry, to the college ministry, never actually engrafting them into the congregation corporately. Then, these same parents are puzzled when, as young adults, their children leave the church. Often, they leave the church because they were never a part of it. They merely trafficked in all the church's group ministries. We should prioritize the corporate gathering of God's people first. The body of Christ is all of God's people, with all our eclectic differences, coming together to serve and worship Jesus.

Cultivate Orderliness

In 1 Timothy 3, Paul says the pastor "must manage his own household competently and have his children under control with all dignity. (If anyone does not know how to manage his own household, how will he take care of God's church?)" (vv. 4–5). Chaos, confusion, and rebellion in the home disqualify an elder from ministry, but they also undermine the testimony of any Christian family, pastor, or laity. There are seasons of life that are especially trying and challenging, but let's strive for a home that reflects order and a biblical pattern.

Practice Family Worship

Do not be intimidated by the phrase "family worship." By this, I simply mean family devotion. In short, reading the Bible, praying, and perhaps singing together. It should not be a daunting task, merely flavoring each day with a few minutes of intentionally focusing your family on Christ and his Word. As Charles Spurgeon wisely observed, "If we want to bring up a godly family, who shall be a seed to serve God when our heads are under the clods of the valley, let us seek to train them up in the fear of God by meeting together as a family for worship."[5]

Demonstrate the Grace of Repentance and Forgiveness

Discipline is not a one-way street. Just as we discipline our children, our heavenly Father disciplines us. When our children sin, we should expect their repentance and grant them grace. When we sin, we should seek our children's forgiveness and grace. Herein, they will learn the gospel way, and we will protect our family from hypocrisy. As David Mathis writes, "It is not a question as to whether we sin against our child. All parents sin against their children. The question is whether we recognize and confess our sin, and ask our children for forgiveness."[6]

Practice Hospitality

As far as the family functioning as a little lighthouse for God's glory, we have to let people into our lives to view it. Hospitality is a lost art, but a standing biblical virtue. Whether your home is large or small, new or old, tidy or messy, open your home and demonstrate the gift of hospitality.

Cultivate a Transgenerational Faith

My goal is not only to see my children follow Christ, but their children, and their children, and on and on as well. Like the psalmist who observed, "But from eternity to eternity the LORD's faithful love is toward those who fear him, and his righteousness toward the grandchildren" (Ps. 103:17). Similarly, we should cultivate a transgenerational faith, one in which we shape our family tree for generations to come. To accomplish this, we must lay a solid foundation. This foundation must be doctrinally sound, built on the Word of God; full of warmth, a true love for Christ; and full of passion, understanding the urgency of the gospel and the Great Commission.

In Conclusion

Perhaps more than any other chapter in this book, I feel the weight of this one. My wife and I have been blessed with five children. They are a constant source of delight, and a constant reminder of the profound stewardship that is mine. Parenting is the most enjoyable and exhilarating responsibility I know. I feel as though I am getting to create, invest, sculpt, build, and nurture all at once.

As we do, we know our greatest responsibility is to tend their hearts. For how we shepherd their hearts not only impacts their lives and our family but the church as well—for generations to come.

This stewardship is, ultimately, a gospel one. By the power of the gospel, we parent as God would have us.

Through the gospel, we give and receive grace in our home, thus flavoring it with Christ. And, as we do, our family projects the gospel to a watching world.

The Gospel &
Your Time

or many evangelical churches, Vacation Bible
School (VBS) is one of the most anticipated
weeks of the year. In fact, I can still recall VBS
weeks I attended as a child. The crafts, the games, the
lessons, and the overall sense of Christian adventure
impacted me deeply.

Years later, as a pastor, I similarly looked forward
to VBS. One has to be coldhearted not to enjoy a church
full of kids learning about Christ and what it means to
follow him. As a pastor, I also learned how VBS pro-
vided an opportunity to not only reach community kids
but their parents as well. Therefore, I always leaned

into Vacation Bible School, expecting God to work in the life of our church.

Seeking a strong turnout, the Saturdays before VBS I would lead teams from our church out into the community, letting our neighbors know about the upcoming week and seeking to "pre-enroll" kids. You quickly learn which doors to knock on. The yards littered with bicycles, tricycles, and toys held promise of kids inside.

I vividly recall one exchange I had with a boy, seven or eight years old, while inviting him to VBS. It was high noon, on a particularly hot summer day. The boy and I both were pouring sweat. We were standing on the front porch of his trailer while I was explaining VBS and leaving a flier for his parents. The boy, gazing up at me, was holding an ice cream cone in his right hand, but I noticed a funny thing. The whole time we talked he never took a lick.

The boy stood there, holding his cone, melting away by the moment, with vanilla ice-cream streaming down his arm. I encouraged him to enjoy it, but he calmly, thoughtfully, said he was saving it for later. I admired his uncommon delayed gratification, but I felt for the boy who was stubbornly trying to stop the unstoppable.

Time Marches On

We live in an age where adults are trying to stop the unstoppable as well—the onward march of time. A cottage industry has sprung up around trying to prolong one's life: extreme fitness, nutritional supplements, human growth hormones, and, most ridiculously, the cryogenics movement. Fitness and healthy living are commendable, but the mind-set that through them you will outpace death is not.

The Bible teaches, emphatically, that we cannot outrun death. As the hymn writer Isaac Watts instructs us, "Time, like an ever-rolling stream, bears all its sons away." The Bible tells us our days are numbered and that we cannot presume upon tomorrow (Job. 14:5). Therefore, we should live with the length of eternity, not the length of our earthly days, on the forefront of our minds. Thus, we are to steward our time like our money—saving it, investing it, and using it, with wisdom and intentionality.

Redeeming Your Time

How we use our time is ultimately a gospel issue. The gospel affects how we view our time on this earth, how we allocate our time, and how we conceptualize eternity. How do we best redeem our time? More important than action steps is our outlook, our basic attitude toward time and eternity.

We must remember, as the apostle Paul teaches us, the days are evil. The apostle writes, "Pay careful attention, then, to how you live—not as unwise people but as wise—making the most of the time, because the days are evil" (Eph. 5:15–16). By this he means that we must live our lives in light of spiritual realities, ministry opportunities, and Great Commission urgencies.

If we rightly think of time and eternity in light of the gospel, the "must-do's" and the "how-to's" will largely take care of themselves. This is to say, when our view of time is right, we are preinclined to making the right day-to-day decisions about how we use it. Thus, viewing our time through a biblical and convictional lens is essential, and that is what we are seeking to do in this chapter.

Reflect on the Brevity of Life and the Length of Eternity

Life passes us by at a shockingly rapid pace. With each passing year, this pace seems to pick up speed. One day our kids are born; the next day they graduate high school. One day we enter the workforce; the next day we retire. One day we stride across the dawn of life; the next day we limp into its sunset.

Psalm 90, a psalm of Moses, captures this reality unlike any other passage. Reflect carefully on these God-inspired words:

> Lord, you have been our refuge
> in every generation.
> Before the mountains were born,

before you gave birth to the earth and the
   world,
from eternity to eternity, you are God.
You return mankind to the dust,
saying, "Return, descendants of Adam."
For in your sight a thousand years
are like yesterday that passes by,
like a few hours of the night.
You end their lives; they sleep.
They are like grass that grows in the
   morning—
in the morning it sprouts and grows;
by evening it withers and dries up.
For we are consumed by your anger;
we are terrified by your wrath.
You have set our iniquities before you,
our secret sins in the light of your presence.
For all our days ebb away under your wrath;
we end our years like a sigh.
Our lives last seventy years
or, if we are strong, eighty years.
Even the best of them are struggle and sorrow;
indeed, they pass quickly and we fly away.
Who understands the power of your anger?
Your wrath matches the fear that is due you.
Teach us to number our days carefully
so that we may develop wisdom in our hearts.
(Ps. 90:1–12)

Note carefully how Moses describes the brevity of life. Our lives last seventy, perhaps eighty or so years, and then we fly away.

Along these lines, David Mathis astutely observed, "You are always on the clock. There's no avoiding it. Every human, in every place on the planet, whatever the culture, is subject to the incessant passing of time. The sands are always falling. No matter how much we neglect it, suppress it, or stress about it, there is nothing we can do to stem the onslaught. Ignore the rush to your own peril. Or walk the path of wisdom in stewarding your short and few days as gifts from God."[1]

Mathis is right, and so we must regularly reflect upon the brevity of life and the length of eternity.

Realize the Uncertainty of Tomorrow

Prudence is a biblical virtue. Presumption is not. We should save, work, plan, and prepare for life's contingencies well into the future. At the same time, we cannot assume we will have a future. Consider what Jesus' brother, James, has to say about this:

> Come now, you who say, "Today or tomorrow we will travel to such and such a city and spend a year there and do business and make a profit." Yet you do not know what tomorrow will bring— what your life will be! For you are like vapor that appears for a little while, then vanishes. Instead,

you should say, "If the Lord wills, we will live and do this or that." But as it is, you boast in your arrogance. All such boasting is evil. So it is sin to know the good and yet not do it. (James 4:13–17)

Our lives being described as a vapor has a sobering effect. Recognize today that you are not promised tomorrow.

As I write this chapter in February 2017, my place of residence, Kansas City, has been jolted by the brevity of life. Our city, and the world of Major League Baseball, was stunned when Yordano Ventura, the Kansas City Royals' star pitcher, was tragically killed in an automobile accident. He was only twenty-five years old, threw a 100- mph fastball, and appeared to own his future. The Royals' manager, Ned Yost, reflected that young star athletes think of themselves as bulletproof, never imagining their life may be cut short.

As Christ-followers, may the same not be said of us. Make every effort to realize the uncertainty of tomorrow.

Remember, Time Is Your Most Precious Possession

Time, not money, is your most precious possession. Yet, we throw our time away in alarming ways. Fiddling on social media, vegging out in front of the television, or just giving huge chunks of time to idle chatter, are all akin to throwing our time away.

Accordingly, Don Whitney observed, "If people threw away their money as thoughtlessly as they throw away their time, we would think them insane. Yet time is infinitely more precious than money because money can't buy time."[2]

Yet, this is not just for our own benefit; it is for that of Christ and his kingdom. Our allotment of time is a special gift from him, for us to use in light of our divine stewardship.

Learn to Say "No"

You will not rightly steward your time until you learn to pronounce the word *no*. For me, saying the word *no* did not come naturally. When pushed, I could spit it out, but I preferred to steer clear of it. I was equipped to say "no" over issues of doctrine, conviction, or morality, but I was much less capable of saying "no" over more subjective, less consequential issues—especially when asked to do something by someone I knew and loved, like family, friends, or fellow church members.

In hindsight, it was not for fear of conflict or reprisal that I tended to go along. I was hesitant to disappoint. I was reluctant to let someone down. The result usually was not disaster, but it often brought about some other downside—a dilution of my time and resources.

Additionally, saying "yes" often curtailed my ability to give time and energy to other, more worthy causes, including my church and my family. Unapologetically, I hoard our family time like a miser, gripping it tightly, and intuitively swatting away opportunities and expectations that would compromise it. The adage is true: when you say "yes" to something, you are saying "no" to something else.

Learn from Jonathan Edwards

The New England minister Jonathan Edwards is considered one of the greatest Christians in church history. His preaching in the 1740s, along with the evangelist George Whitefield, ushered in the Great Awakening and helped to found our country on a Christian footing.

Edwards was a prolific theologian, philosopher, preacher, and author. The *Encyclopedia Britannica* cites Edwards as the greatest mind America ever produced. When he died from an experimental small pox vaccination at the age of fifty-four, he had just been appointed president of the College of New Jersey, which would come to be known as Princeton University.

Countless studies have been undertaken on Edwards, seeking the secret of his success. Invariably, these studies cite seventy resolutions Edwards drafted as a young man, in his late teens and early twenties. Many of Edwards's resolutions considered the preciousness of time and his intentionality to maximize it.

Consider a few of them:

- Resolution 5: "Resolved, never to lose one moment of time; but improve it the most profitable way I can."
- Resolution 7: "Resolved, never to do anything, which I should be afraid to do, if it were the last hour of my life."
- Resolution 17: "Resolved, that I will live so as I shall wish I had done when I come to die."
- Resolution 41: "Resolved, to ask myself at the end of every day, week, month, and year, wherein I could possibly in any respect have done better."
- Resolution 50: "Resolved, I will act so as I think I shall judge would have been best, and most prudent, when I come into the future world."
- Resolution #52: "I frequently hear persons in old age say how they would live, if they were to live their lives over again: Resolved, that I will live just so as I can think I had done, supposing I live to old age."[3]

Granted, you may be thinking, *I am no Jonathan Edwards. And he was too uptight, anyway.* The point is not that we must emulate him. The point is that we would do well, in our own lives and contexts, to think more, not less, on these things. Surely none of us, in our final days, will complain of having been too intentional with our time.

In Conclusion

Of all the chapters in this book, the gospel and my time has been most on my mind of late. While writing this book, I turned forty. I am now officially over the proverbial hill. I have not yet had a "mid-life crisis," and I am not intending to have one. But crossing this milestone has prompted sober reflection, a taking of stock in my life.

What did I turn up? Well, this I know: I am not guaranteed a tomorrow, but, if actuarial tables are correct and I enjoy a standard, projected lifespan, then I am roughly halfway home. And, the second half will pass much more quickly than the first.

Therefore as followers of Christ, we should recognize that the gospel radically affects the way we view our time and how we spend it. What we do *in time* will greatly affect us when we are *out of time*.

Thus, I rededicated myself to living in light of the couplet I learned as a new believer, a couplet you also would do well to live by: "Only one life, twill soon be past; only what's done for Christ will last."[4]

The Gospel & Your Money

D id you know that Jesus spoke more about money than any other topic? That's right. In fact, sixteen of Christ's thirty-eight parables reference our handling of earthly treasure. In the Gospels, one out of every ten verses when Jesus is speaking addresses money. As John Piper observed, "Jesus spoke more about money than he did about sex, heaven, and hell. Money is a big deal to Jesus."[1]

I learned long ago that what is important to Jesus ought to be important to me. If this principle is true, then we must think intentionally about money, just as he did. If Jesus died to redeem every aspect of us—as we mentioned before—then the gospel affects our pocketbooks. As his gospel transforms our life, he transforms our view of money—and its use.

So, why did Jesus focus on money? Because money is a gauge, an indicator that reveals a thousand data points about our hearts. Our view of money uncovers our motives, our ambitions, our insecurities, our greed, and our internal value system. Few things reveal our hearts like our money does.

Money can also be corrosive—at least the love of money can be. The love of money will decay our hearts, pollute our ambitions, and stain our Christian lives.

Yet, money is also a tool, when rightly utilized, that can bring about much good. Money rightly stewarded can provide for our families, support our churches, bless Christian ministries, care for the needy, and generate a host of other biblical and practical goods.

Considering Key Passages

As noted, Jesus focused on earthly treasure and godly stewardship, but so did other biblical authors. In fact, stewardship is one of the Bible's most common themes. Let's reflect on a couple of major, heart-shaping passages on money.

Consider the words of Christ:

"Don't store up for yourselves treasures on earth, where moth and rust destroy and where thieves break in and steal. But store up for yourselves treasures in heaven, where neither moth nor rust destroys, and where thieves don't break in or steal. For where your treasure is, there your heart will be also." (Matt. 6:19–21)

"No servant can serve two masters, since either he will hate one and love the other, or he will be devoted to one and despise the other. You cannot serve both God and money." The Pharisees, who were lovers of money, were listening to all these things and scoffing at him. And he told them, "You are the ones who justify yourselves in the sight of others, but God knows your hearts. For what is highly admired by people is revolting in God's sight." (Luke 16:13–15)

Additionally, the apostle Paul warns us:

But godliness with contentment is great gain. For we brought nothing into the world, and we can take nothing out. If we have food and clothing, we will be content with these. But those who want to be rich fall into temptation, a trap, and many foolish and harmful desires, which plunge people into ruin and destruction. For the love of money is a root of all kinds of evil, and by craving it, some have wandered away from the faith and pierced themselves with many griefs. (1 Tim. 6:6–10)

Instruct those who are rich in the present age not to be arrogant or to set their hope on the uncertainty of wealth, but on God, who richly provides us with all things to enjoy. Instruct them to do what is good, to be rich in good works, to be generous and willing to share, storing up treasure for themselves as a good foundation for the coming age, so that they may take hold of what is truly life. (1 Tim. 6:17–19)

And, lastly, the author of Hebrews says, "Keep your life free from the love of money. Be satisfied with what you have, for he himself has said, 'I will never leave you or abandon you'" (Heb. 13:5).

With these passages in mind, how should we view money? How should we evaluate earthly wealth? What does it mean for the gospel to redeem our pocket books? How can you honor God with your earthly resources? As we consider these questions, know the stakes are high.

Let's focus on seven principles of a redeemed approach to money. And as we do, remember Billy Graham's observation: "If a person gets his attitude toward money straight, it will help straighten out almost every other area in his life."[2]

Don't Love the Provision, Love the Provider

One of the reassuring realities of the Christian life is God's scrupulous care and lavish generosity on his children. Not only is he able to care for us; he is committed to doing so. Not only is he willing to bless us; he delights in it. As Jesus taught:

> "Consider the birds of the sky: They don't sow or reap or gather into barns, yet your heavenly Father feeds them. Aren't you worth more than they? Can any of you add one moment to his lifespan by worrying? And why do you worry about clothes? Observe how the wildflowers of the field grow: They don't labor or spin thread. Yet I tell you that not even Solomon in all his splendor was adorned like one of these. If that's how God clothes the grass of the field, which is here today and thrown into the furnace tomorrow, won't he do much more for you—you of little faith? So don't worry, saying, 'What will we eat?' or 'What will we drink?' or 'What will we wear?' For the Gentiles eagerly seek all these things, and your heavenly Father knows that you need them. But seek first the kingdom of God and his righteousness, and all these things will be provided for you." (Matt. 6:26–33)

The sparkling reality of the Christian life is that God not only meets our needs but often far surpasses them. As he provides, we must worship the Provider. As he gives, sure, we can enjoy the gift, but we should delight in the Giver most of all.

Pursue Contentment More Than Gain

This is key, as the apostle Paul teaches us: "Godliness with contentment is great gain" (1 Tim. 6:6). The reality is, discontentment is like a leaking basin that can never be filled regardless of how much water you put into it. Conversely, contentment is like an artesian well, never running dry regardless of how much you take out.

I love how Paul David Tripp frames this reality. He writes, "Love of money is really about contentment. Love of money is about humility. Love of money is about identity. Love of money is about worship that really roots at deep issues. Maybe the most subtle of the indications of love of money is an ongoing, chronic discontentment in me that, no matter what I have, I am still not content."[3]

Realize that in Christ, you have all you need. Be content in him.

View All That You Have through the Prism of Stewardship

Stewardship is a concept we are all familiar with, but perhaps not as much as we should be. To be a steward is to recognize that we are not the owners of our possessions—just temporary overseers. We will be judged by rightly stewarding—storing up for ourselves treasure in heaven.

Ray Ortlund adds an interesting twist to this concept, one that illumines and accentuates our responsibility:

> We are accustomed to the biblical message that we should trust God. But here is another—smaller and subordinate, but still important—category: that God would trust us. If we are not faithful (*pistoi*) with money, which is unrighteous and not worth much, who will entrust (*pisteusei*) to us the true riches of spiritual wealth and power? In other words, if we can't handle cheap things wisely, why would God put far more precious things into our hands?[4]

Are you being a faithful steward over what God has entrusted to you?

Prioritize Giving to God

Over the years, I have heard church members insist they will start giving to God when they can afford it. That thinking is not only unbiblical but also foolish. That is like a young, married couple saying, "We will have a baby—once we can afford it." That type of thinking will leave you without children—and without giving.

Delayed obedience is always disobedience, including with our money. One of the most alarming passages in the Bible is Malachi 3:7–10. Consider God's warning:

"Since the days of your fathers, you have turned from my statutes; you have not kept them. Return to me, and I will return to you," says the LORD of Armies.

Yet you ask, "How can we return?"

"Will a man rob God? Yet you are robbing me!"

"How do we rob you?" you ask.

"By not making the payments of the tenth and the contributions. You are suffering under a curse, yet you—the whole nation—are still robbing me. Bring the full tenth into the storehouse so that there may be food in my house. Test me in this way," says the LORD of Armies. "See if I will not open the floodgates of heaven and pour out a blessing for you without measure." (Mal. 3:7–10)

Herein is a pitfall many Christians fall into. They view 10 percent as a spiritual tax, one that they should give to God and then proceed to do as they will with the rest. But biblical stewardship teaches us that God doesn't own 10 percent of our money; he owns all of it. As we look to the New Testament, especially the apostle Paul's teaching, we find an emphasis on grace giving, which reframes our thinking. I would encourage you not to view 10 percent as a ceiling, but a floor, and seek his will as to strategic, kingdom opportunities within and beyond your church.

Forget Not God's Provisions

In the Old Testament, God's people strove not to forget his provision. They often built artifacts of remembrance, erected altars, consecrated tabernacles and other objects to remind them of God's care. We should do that as well.

Over the years, when God has answered a financial prayer, my wife and I have journaled it, seeking to never forget it. This was especially true in the early years of our marriage. Seminary studies, a small church pastorate, and a growing family meant times were occasionally tight. On numerous occasions, God answered specific financial prayer requests. Requests that were urgent and prompted by true need. As God responded, we journaled those stories of his provision and have placed in our lives strategic reminders of God's goodness. Now that our kids are older, we reflect on those times as a family. As we do, it strengthens our faith and teaches our children how God provides.

Value Working, Saving, and Investing

Sometimes the most spiritual thing you can do is also the most practical. While we are called to be people of faith, we also are called to diligence, labor, and prudence. Paul exhorted Christians that if they did not work they should not eat (2 Thess. 3:10), and not taking care of one's family is worse than unbelief (1 Tim. 5:8).

Likewise, Proverbs commends both saving and investing, giving us principles like:

- The plans of the diligent lead surely to advantage, but everyone who is hasty comes surely to poverty (Prov. 21:5).
- Wealth obtained by fraud dwindles, but the one who gathers by labor increases it (Prov. 13:11).

In fact, the Bible consistently praises hard work, careful planning, and wise financial stewardship. Christianity is not a "get rich" scheme. That is, in part, why the prosperity gospel is such a big, fat lie. You know the prosperity gospel, right? The slick televangelist who says if you send him your money, God will make you rich. I always wonder why the televangelist doesn't send us his money, and let God make him rich? If he really believed his lie, he would choose to be the beneficiary of it.

Cultivate the Heart of a Cheerful Giver

From my years as a pastor and from serving in seminary contexts, I have seen cheerful givers up close. They are a remarkable breed of people—those who have found the joy of giving. They love to give—relishing the ability to bless God's causes and God's people. This is more than a personality trait—it is a Christian distinctive, one that is commended by God, and one we are called to cultivate. As Paul told the church at Corinth, "Each person should do as he has decided in his heart—not reluctantly or out of compulsion, since God loves a cheerful giver" (2 Cor. 9:7).

In Conclusion

Given my audience in this book, I know I am writing primarily to American Christians, which makes the issue of money all the more urgent. We are a fabulously wealthy nation. In fact, one can argue we are the wealthiest nation in the history of humanity, ranking us among the most affluent Christians of all time. The allure of money is ever present, as are the temptations that can come with it.

Therefore, we must keep Christ's warning ever before us: "For what will it benefit someone if he gains the whole world yet loses his life? Or what will anyone give in exchange for his life?" (Matt. 16:26). Let's not negotiate away our spiritual inheritance or compromise our Christian convictions or gospel testimony. Let's view our money as God does—as a redeemed asset—and purpose to steward it accordingly. As we do, our money will be a vehicle for God's glory in our lives.

The Gospel &
Your Work

W hat do you want to be when you grow up?"
That question, which is so common today,
would be shockingly irrelevant for the vast
majority of humans who have ever lived.

In the premodern world, one's work usually was
not a matter of choice. It was essential to one's identity.
It was more a matter of who you were than what you
did. Let's consider farming, for example. Farming was
not merely what one did; a farmer was who you were.
It was just as much a matter of one's identity as it was
one's activity.

If your father and his forebears had been farmers for
generations on end, you would most likely become the

same. You would till the land and husband its resources like your predecessors did, and your descendants would likely follow after you. In the post-Industrial Era, work took on a different aspect, and the sense of calling and pride in one's work—which often accompanied it—gave way to more practical considerations. Hence, many men took factory jobs in the twentieth century, not because they felt called to manufacture widgets on an assembly line but because they wanted to provide a steady income and health insurance for their families. The end of their work was no less noble, even if the means to provide for their families wasn't particularly a matter of pride.

For Christians, though, as we will see, God created us to work. It is the context in which we spend the bulk of our adult lives, and it is the primary arena in which we can glorify Christ. And as we work intentionally for God's glory, our work lives can become a potent gospel witness.

So how does the gospel specifically affect our work? To be able to answer this question correctly, we must first get a biblical understanding of what work is.

A Brief Theology of Work

Many Christians wrongly believe that work is a consequence of Adam's sin in the garden, and that in heaven we will be free from effort and exertion. Nothing could be further from the truth. Adam had a job description before he and Eve fell into sin. God instructed the couple to husband the land, exercise dominion over his creatures, and to steward the creation entrusted to them. Consider the creation account of Genesis 1:

> Then God said, "Let us make man in our image, according to our likeness. They will rule the fish of the sea, the birds of the sky, the livestock, the whole earth, and the creatures that crawl on the earth."
>
> > So God created man
> > in his own image;
> > he created him in the image of God;
> > he created them male and female.
>
> > God blessed them, and God said to them, "Be fruitful, multiply, fill the earth, and subdue it. Rule the fish of the sea, the birds of the sky, and every creature that crawls on the earth." (Gen. 1:26–28)

Did you see all God commanded of Adam? He told Adam to "*rule* the fish of the sea" and then he instructed Adam and Eve to "be *fruitful, multiply, fill the earth, and subdue it*" and, ultimately, to "*rule . . . every creature that crawls on the earth.*" God's instructions are thorough and detailed, telling Adam exactly what he is to be busy doing. It sounds like a demanding job description to me!

Similarly, at the end of the age, we will have assignments in heaven. We will not be floating to and fro on clouds, enjoying uninterrupted rest and leisure. We will be worshiping Christ, exercising care over delegated responsibilities, and co-reigning with him for all eternity.

As Jim Hamilton writes, in the new heavens and new earth,

> God will bring to pass the purposes he set out to achieve when he spoke the world into existence. . . . God will make the world new, and we will do new work.
>
> The new work we will do is the work of ruling and subduing, working and keeping, exercising dominion and rendering judgment, all as God's people in God's place in God's way.[1]

Work Versus Toil

Now, it is true that in the meantime, and due to Adam's fall, our work has become toilsome. Originally, as we have seen, God intended Adam to work, to exercise authority, and to fulfill God's divine purposes for his creation. Adam's sin corrupted every aspect of his life, including his work life. In short, his work became toil.

Again, let's return to Genesis and consider God's curse on Adam.

And he said to the man, "Because you listened to your wife and ate from the tree about which I commanded you, 'Do not eat from it':

The ground is cursed because of you.
You will eat from it by means of painful
    labor
all the days of your life.
It will produce thorns and thistles for you,
and you will eat the plants of the field.
You will eat bread by the sweat of your
    brow
until you return to the ground,
since you were taken from it.
For you are dust,
and you will return to dust." (Gen. 3:17–19)

What is going on here? What is the difference between work and toil? Leeland Ryken helps us understand this distinction:

The Fall did not introduce work into the world. Work as a blessing was already present. The new element is that work has now become a curse. It is, more specifically, a punishment that people bear as a burden. Something that was originally good has been perverted from its original perfection.

In other words, work has become toil—something that must be accomplished against the hostility of the environment in which work occurs. Work originally served a purpose of human fulfillment, but it is now a source of frustration. W. R. Forrester comments that "man was meant to be a gardener, but by reason of his sin he became a farmer."[2]

So, after the Fall, work became toil—something sweaty, exertive, often painful, and occurring outside the perfect, comfortable context of the garden of Eden. Like every other dimension of our lives, Adam's sin corrupted our work.

Reconsidering Vocation

At this point, we should consider another important aspect of our work—the concept of vocation. During the Middle Ages, a class distinction emerged between the clergy and laity, which recognized the former as more noble, desirable, and beneficial than the latter.

During the Protestant Reformation, Martin Luther, along with other Reformers, reasserted the biblical concept of vocation and argued that God extends two calls on a person's life. One, a general call to follow Christ; another, a call to a specific vocation, or work. We know our vocational call by gifting, ability, and opportunity, and we both honor God and serve man as we fulfill it.

Thus, our vocational lives are a key component of our Christian identity and Christian witness. Consider Gene Veith on this point:

> The ability to read God's Word is an inexpressibly precious blessing, but reading is an ability that did not spring fully formed in our young minds, it required the *vocation* of teachers. God protects us through the cop on the beat and the whole panoply of the legal system. He gives us beauty and meaning through artists. He lets us travel through the ministry of auto workers, mechanics, road crews, and airline employees. He keeps us clean through the work of garbage collectors, plumbers, sanitation workers, and sometimes undocumented aliens who clean our hotel rooms. He brings people to salvation through pastors and through anyone else who proclaims the Gospel of Jesus Christ to the lost. The fast-food worker, the inventor; the clerical assistant, the scientist; the accountant, the musician—they all have high callings, used by God to bless and serve His people and His creation.[3]

Therefore, as a Christian, even if you are independently wealthy, you are still called to lead a productive life. Endless days of sun tanning, golfing, and, as John Piper has lamented, "sea-shell collecting," are vacuous if they become the end goal of your life. In order to glorify God through your work and in retirement, your steady productivity is imperative.

The point is not that it is dishonorable to retire. The point is that even in our retirement we are to live in a way that is productive, Christ-honoring, and given to our families and our churches. In other words, regardless of our life-stage, we are called to honor Christ through what we do and how we do it.

God has indeed made us, by gifting and by calling, for certain tasks. As we fulfill those tasks, we flourish, our families are strengthened, others are well served, and Christ is honored. We need, then, to discover and pursue our vocation.

As Keith Welton encourages us, "Our hands are the instruments of our heart. They express outwardly what we believe inwardly. Our work ought to show we have a higher calling. It ought to say that something greater than earthly reward motivates it. The quality of our work should glorify God."[4]

How, then, should we view our work? How does the gospel impact our work? Let's take a look at five keys to focus upon as we go about our work life.

Work as Unto the Lord

For God to be honored in our work, we have to work unto the Lord. We are to view him as our ultimate source of accountability. We, in a sense, are his employees—we serve unto him. Scripture charges us in exactly this way.

- "So, whether you eat or drink, or whatever you do, do everything to the glory of God" (1 Cor. 10:31).
- "Whatever you do, do it from the heart, as something done for the Lord and not for people, knowing that you will receive the reward of an inheritance from the Lord. You serve the Lord Christ" (Col. 3:23–24).

We glorify the Lord through our work by living out the Christian life, and its expected virtues, in the arena of our occupation. A Christian who is honest and diligent, who avoids gossip and greed in the workplace provides a sharp contrast with our dog-eat-dog world. As Marshall Segal noted, "Where you work is not nearly as important as why you work."[5]

Cultivate Productivity

God made us as cyclical creatures, rhythmically designed for work, recreation, and rest. This pattern reminds us that we serve an infinite God, but we are finite creatures. Our daily dependence on sleep and our ongoing need for rest and recreation teach us of our dependence on the Lord and, metaphorically, of the spiritual rest we find in Christ.

Yet, we must be careful that our rest does not morph into slothfulness; that our recreation does not become a preoccupation with leisure. The following proverbs warn us accordingly:

- "The slacker craves, yet has nothing, but the diligent is fully satisfied" (Prov. 13:4).
- "The diligent hand will rule, but laziness will lead to forced labor" (Prov. 12:24).
- "There is profit in all hard work, but endless talk leads only to poverty" (Prov. 14:23).

God designed us to be productive creatures, intentionally fulfilling the responsibilities entrusted to us. That is why, oddly, productivity is a form of rest. We can identify with John Piper, who famously reflected, "Productivity is restful to my soul."[6]

Work for Pay

The Bible emphasizes the importance of working as a means to provide for ourselves and our family. We honor the Scriptures and reflect God's glory when we fulfill this simple expectation—we earn our pay. Again, let's consider the Bible's teachings:

- "But if anyone does not provide for his own family, especially for his own household, he has denied the faith and is worse than an unbeliever" (1 Tim. 5:8).
- "Seek to lead a quiet life, to mind your own business, and to work with your own hands, as we commanded you, so that you may behave properly in the presence of outsiders and not be dependent on anyone" (1 Thess. 4:11–12).
- "We exhort you, brothers and sisters: warn those who are idle, comfort the discouraged, help the weak, be patient with everyone" (1 Thess. 5:14).
- "When we were with you, this is what we commanded you: 'If anyone isn't willing to work, he should not eat.' For we hear that there are some among you who are idle. They are not busy but busybodies. Now we command and exhort such people by the Lord Jesus Christ to work quietly and provide for themselves" (2 Thess. 3:10–12).

Why does the Bible so emphasize the importance of work and of earning one's sustenance? Because it is good for all parties. For the individual, it enables them to fulfill God's creative order, which gives the individual a sense of purpose, productivity, and fulfillment. It is also good for others, including church and society. If you subsidize people who simply choose not to work, you dilute the available resources for those who are truly in need: the sick, aged, and indigent.

Pay for Work

Not only are we to work for our pay, but for those on the other side of the equation, we are to pay for work rendered for us. Again, we are called in Scripture to demonstrate wise stewardship but also just compensation and even Christian generosity.

- "For the Scripture says, 'Do not muzzle the ox while it is treading out the grain,' and the worker is worthy of his wages" (1 Tim. 5:18).
- "The hardworking farmer ought to be the first to get a share of the crops" (2 Tim. 2:6).

Our handling of money indicates much about the authenticity of our Christian witness. If we delay payment, shortchange, or finagle people over money, it undermines our testimony. Whether tipping a restaurant server or paying your own employees, let's do so unto the Lord.

See Your Job as a Gospel Platform

Finally, understand that, as an adult, your job is where you spend the bulk of your daylight hours. Do not fall into the mind-set that your Monday-through-Saturday life is secular, divorced from your Sunday life. Understand your work life, when lived with a redemptive purpose, is an awesome platform for the gospel of Christ.

Popular Christian author Tim Keller made this very case in his book *Every Good Endeavor.* In it, he rightly observed, "Christians who grasp a biblical theology of work learn not only to value and participate in the work of all people but to also see ways to work distinctively as Christians."[7] Let's make sure we cultivate this mind-set in our lives and in our work.

In Conclusion

I am one of those blessed individuals who absolutely loves what God has called him to do. I feel profoundly centered in his will and deeply satisfied in the calling God has placed on my life.

The Christian Olympian, Eric Liddell, famously testified that he felt God's pleasure when he ran. I feel God's pleasure as I serve Midwestern Seminary. As I often tell my trustees, "I love my job so much, I would do it for free—but let's not get crazy about it."

May the Lord grant you similar satisfaction and, as you enjoy it, may you purpose to work for his glory, as unto him.

The Gospel & Your Recreation

Every man needs a hero, and Winston Churchill is one of mine. Churchill, Great Britain's iconic wartime prime minister, consistently ranks as one of the greatest Englishman who ever lived. And rightly so.

Born in 1874, Churchill came of age in the Victorian Era, and he served the British Empire at its zenith. From boyhood, Churchill dreamed of grandeur, desiring to be like his ancestor, John Churchill, the Duke of Marlborough, who led his country victoriously through the War of Spanish Succession. In the crucible of World War II, Winston Churchill would have his opportunity.

Churchill was a bulldog; he resolutely led his people in defiance of Adolph Hitler. Under Churchill's leadership, the British people withstood the Germans' constant air bombing of their homeland and were prepared to resist to the death an impending Nazi invasion. In the end, he led his people to victory.

Churchill is most commonly remembered for his wartime leadership, but he was truly a Renaissance man, one who excelled in many different areas of life. He was a decorated soldier, an accomplished war correspondent, a public intellectual, a Pulitzer Prize-winning author, an award-winning artist, and a moving orator.

What is more, Churchill held a seat in the British Parliament for sixty-three years and notably served in various governmental offices, including two distinguished stints as the British prime minister.

Less known is how much Churchill enjoyed working with his hands. He cared for animals, oversaw construction projects at his country home, Chartwell, and even earned a masonry license from his local union.

Churchill appreciated the biblical balances of work and rest, of vocation and recreation, of labor and leisure. He once mused that a person who worked with his mind needed a hobby that used his hands, and a person who worked with his hands needed a hobby that used his mind.

This cycle, Churchill observed, brought balance, renewal, and growth to one's life. Churchill, intentionally or not, brushed up against a biblical pattern of work and rest, of exertion and renewal.

Work and Recreation in the Old Testament

Throughout the Old Testament, we see a consistent work-rest pattern. It begins by God's example in the created order. Recall how God created for six days, declared it good, and rested on the seventh.

> So the heavens and the earth and everything in them were completed. On the seventh day God had completed his work that he had done, and he rested on the seventh day from all his work that he had done. God blessed the seventh day and declared it holy, for on it he rested from all his work of creation. (Gen. 2:1–3)

Here we note, God's rest was not due to fatigue, but for reflection, satisfaction, and celebration. The principle holds for us as well. We are not merely to rest and recreate as needed, but more rhythmically, and for a host of reasons, as we shall see.

But first, back to the creation narrative. Know that the divine pattern of work and rest begins at creation, but it does not end there. The work-rest continuum was so important that God enshrined it in the Ten Commandments, insisting that his people:

> Remember the Sabbath day, to keep it holy. You are to labor six days and do all your work, but the seventh day is a Sabbath to the LORD your God. You must not do any work—you, your son

or daughter, your male or female servant, your livestock, or the resident alien who is within your city gates. For the LORD made the heavens and the earth, the sea, and everything in them in six days; then he rested on the seventh day. Therefore the LORD blessed the Sabbath day and declared it holy. (Exod. 20:8–11)

Work and Recreation in the New Testament

In the New Testament, the Sabbath principle is maintained, but the Sabbath as a day to be strictly observed is not. In fact, each one of the Ten Commandments is restated in the New Testament, except the fourth, to keep the Sabbath. The apostle Paul instructed believers that they were free from keeping "diets and days," and we see the church gathering not on the sixth day, but the seventh, the Lord's Day.

Yet, there is a principle that carries forward. The author of Hebrews tells us that we, as believers, enter into a perfect rest. But it is not by a day; it is through a person—Jesus Christ. The Sabbath day foreshadowed the rest believers find in Christ. It is a relief from our religious works, from our spiritual striving, and a rest in the finished work of Jesus Christ.

Though the day foreshadowed a person, Jesus, we are still left with the Lord's Day as an institution in order to prioritize corporate worship, fellowship with

God's people, and rest. We are left with the sabbatical principle, which runs throughout Scripture, that we are to balance lives of work and productivity with rest and recreation.

We see this pattern in the life of Christ and his disciples. Jesus lived with constant pressure. There were always multitudes to feed, the infirmed to heal, and crowds to teach. From an earthly standpoint, Jesus had a never-ending to-do list. Yet, Mark tells us, "Very early in the morning, while it was still dark, he got up, went out, and made his way to a deserted place; and there he was praying." (Mark 1:35). Did you see that? After a busy season of ministry (as the preceding verses make clear), Jesus pulled away for solitude and renewal.

Similarly, later in Mark, Jesus instructed his disciples to do the same. Jesus said to them, "'Come away by yourselves to a remote place and rest for a while.' For many people were coming and going, and they did not even have time to eat" (Mark 6:31).

So, realize that you honor the Lord by enjoying seasons of rest and recreation. Taking a break is not an interruption to the Christian life; it *is* the Christian life. Sometimes the most spiritual thing you can do is take a nap.

If, then, the work-rest pattern is a biblical and healthy practice for every Christian, how do we practice it? Moreover, how does the gospel affect our rest? How can we recreate for the glory of God?

Honor the Lord's Day

As we have seen, the Lord's Day does not hold the same force and detailed expectations that the Sabbath once did. Yet, in our aim to correct, let's be careful not to overcorrect. Let's make sure we honor the Lord's Day. We can accomplish this in a number of way.

First, prioritize gathering with God's people for Lord's Day worship. Plan your weekend around Sundays, striving not to interfere with them. As the author of Hebrews warns us, "Let us consider how to stimulate one another to love and good deeds, not forsaking our own assembling together, as is the habit of some, but encouraging one another; all the more as you see the day drawing near" (Heb. 10:24–25 NASB).

Secondly, though we are not bound by Sabbatarian expectations, the Lord's Day is a natural day for Sabbath rest. If we do not rest on Sundays, when will we? There is still enough residual cultural-Christianity that society often keeps Sundays free from work expectations and activities. Take advantage of this for your own rest and recreation.

Thirdly, use your added time on Sunday for family togetherness, reading Christian literature, enjoying God's creation through outdoor activities, and the like. Truly, Sunday ought to be our most prized day of the week.

Simplify Your Life

Many Christians do not enjoy rest and recreation because they cannot. A host of factors contribute to this. For some, material excesses force them to work nonstop to pay the bills. For others, an overdone drivenness pushes them to work too much—compromising their health, family, and spiritual lives.

Still others, seeking to raise perfect children, shuttle their kids to and from sports leagues, practices, lessons, etc., disrupting norms of family life. Ultimately parents are most responsible for stewarding their children's hearts, not their batting averages, violin proficiency, or GPA.

Again, we must remember that our days are short, and we are responsible for how we use our time. As the apostle Paul warns us, "Pay careful attention, then, to how you live—not as unwise people but as wise—making the most of the time, because the days are evil" (Eph. 5:15–16).

Unapologetically—as I've mentioned previously in this book—I hoard our family time like a miser, gripping it tightly, and swatting away opportunities and expectations that would compromise it. My wife and I regularly review our calendars, set family priorities accordingly, and intentionally prune activities or commitments that clutter our lives. I would encourage you to do the same—simplify your life!

Redeem Your Recreation

In his helpful book, *Leisure and Spirituality: Biblical, Historical, and Contemporary Perspective,* author Paul Heintzman lists toxins that pollute Christian leisure. His list includes:

- A strong performance and work orientation that neglects God's grace.
- Over-consumption of goods and services that distract us from God and his creation.
- Busyness in leisure activities that prevents us from developing the qualitative dimension of leisure.
- An entertainment culture that overstimulates us and diverts us from finding our true refuge in God and his love.
- An overemphasis upon competitive rather than cooperative activities, organized rather than unstructured play, and spectating rather than participating.[1]

For Christians, this should not be the case. We are to enjoy our recreation and to redeem it for the glory of God. Indeed, our recreation holds promise for the gospel.

How, then, can we redeem our recreation? How can we enjoy our recreation to the glory of God? Consider the following four ways.

Recreate for the Glory of God

Again, reflect on these Scriptural charges:

- "Whatever you do, in word or deed, do everything in the name of the Lord Jesus, giving thanks to God the Father through him" (Col. 3:17).
- "So, whether you eat or drink, or whatever you do, do everything for the glory of God" (1 Cor. 10:31).

As John Piper argues, we glorify God through our recreation by making him an explicit part of it. Piper observes:

Therefore, as we pursue our recreation, let's pursue it to the glory of God. Since God wills recreation, he also wills to be in on it. It is crazy to think that God would create in us certain desires, ordain the innocent means of satisfying them and then spoil the whole thing if we pause to ask his blessing on it.

On the contrary, he will *not* spoil the fun; he will enlarge it and purify it, so we don't go home feeling crummy about how we acted. He will transform the game into a little slice of joyful life and turn the field into a diamond of grace.[2]

Rightly Prioritize Your Recreation

As one wit observed, the average American "worships his work, works at his play, and plays at his worship."[3] Our recreation is not to be job-like, and it certainly is not to be worship-like.

Our recreation should not displace our families or our work, and certainly not our worship. We can, however, pursue our recreation with joy, understanding that God has given it to us for our health and well-being. And, whether it is fishing, exercising, or some other sport or craft, how we engage it reflects on our Christian life. As Joe Thorn observed,

> We abuse the gift of recreation when we live for it, rather than use it to live. Recreation is abused when it dominates our thoughts and time; when it overtakes its proper boundaries. It is used well when it is received with thankfulness, enjoyed in faith, and experienced as a means to a better end.[4]

Think Evangelistically about Your Recreation

I am all for churches building Christian Life Centers and using them for intercongregational activities, but our recreation can be a unique arena for the gospel. For many of us, our recreation is our most consistent interaction with unbelievers. How we conduct ourselves, how we engage people, and the general witness we share and reflect can all be powerful gospel witnesses.

This is when evangelism tends to be most effective, anyway. Usually, it is not through cold-calling a list of church prospects. Usually, it is through engaging unbelievers, on their terms, as we go through our day-to-day lives.

Rest from Your Striving

Moving more specifically to our spiritual lives, the author of Hebrews teaches us that the Sabbath day had a typological dimension—it foreshadowed the rest we have in Christ. When we become believers, we no longer carry the burden of trying to earn our salvation through keeping the law, through our personal morality, or through our religious works and good deeds.

On the contrary, Christ has accomplished our redemption for us. We now serve out of love and unto love. We now practice our Christianity from a position of acceptance, not in order to be accepted. Thus, we can rest in Christ and be spiritually, eternally satisfied in him.

In Conclusion

One of the most driven and productive persons who ever lived was the Protestant Reformer, Martin Luther. Luther was a titanic intellect, a lion in the pulpit, and a relentless servant of Christ. Through his *95 Theses*, his fiery preaching, and tireless pen, Luther challenged the Roman Catholic Church, ushered in biblical reformation and revival, and literally changed the world.

Yet, Luther's secret, by his own admission, was not in his own gifting or determination. It was not even long days and short nights. It was the power of the Word and Spirit of God. Luther testified that he unleashed the Word and then he rested. Luther wrote:

> Take me, for example. I opposed indulgences and all papists, but never by force. I simply taught, preached, wrote God's Word: otherwise I did nothing. And then, while I slept or drank Wittenberg beer with my [friends] Philip and Amsdorf, the Word so greatly weakened the papacy that never a prince or emperor did such damage to it. I did nothing: the Word did it all.[5]

May we, like Luther, be content to fulfill what God has called us unto—nothing less, but nothing more—and then rest in his goodness and in the quiet confidence that he will take our meager efforts and multiply them to his ends. As we live with this confidence, we can work, rest, worship, and recreate, for his glory and for our own well-being.

The Gospel & Your Mind

Christianity is a heart religion. In fact, the Bible refers to conversion as the "circumcision of the heart" (Rom. 2:29). As believers, we speak of inviting Jesus into our hearts. And, as more than one preacher has promised, "Jesus will give you a new heart for a new start."

Additionally, one way we know the power of a sermon is its effect on the heart. At Pentecost, in Acts 2, after the apostle Peter delivered one of the most powerful sermons in church history, the crowd was "pierced to the heart" (Acts 2:37).

St. Augustine famously observed, "Thou hast made us for thyself, Oh Lord, and our *hearts* are restless until they rest in thee."[1] That happens at conversion. Our hearts are satisfied, completely and eternally, through Christ. We then enjoy the inner peace we feel as we worship, pray, and draw near to God.

So, the gospel renews our heart, but it also renews our mind—and more so than most Christians realize. Like every other aspect of our lives, our minds are fallen, darkened by sin, and must be redeemed. The gospel does just that.

The Greatest Commandment

Did you ever notice the "Greatest Commandment" includes your mind? Recall the context. In the Gospels, the Pharisees repeatedly sought to entrap Jesus. They tried to ensnare him in complex, unanswerable questions. The Pharisees posed first-century versions of twenty-first-century trick questions, like the famous, "Have you stopped beating your wife yet?" Either answer is problematic, implying guilt.

One such trick question the Pharisees posed to Christ pertained to the Greatest Commandment. The Pharisees were fascinated with the law, frantically trying to keep it. As they did, they cultivated a polished, external self-righteousness. To onlookers, they appeared righteous and in good standing before God and man, yet their hearts were far from God.

One such question posed by the Pharisees is recorded in multiple Gospels. It had to do with the Greatest Commandment. That is to say, the commandment which ought to be prioritized above all others, the one most urgently to be kept.

> When the Pharisees heard that [Jesus] had silenced the Sadducees, they came together. And one of them, an expert in the law, asked a question to test him: "Teacher, which command in the law is the greatest?" He said to him, 'Love the Lord your God with all your heart, with all your soul, and with all your mind.' This is the greatest and most important command." (Matt. 22:34–38)

Interestingly, in Jesus' answer he synthesized much of the Old Testament law. He rightly prioritizes the inner person, the heart. Yet, he also calls us to love God with all of our minds. Jesus, who pulled no punches when confronting the Pharisees, also called them to love God with their minds. The Pharisees seemed to have this part down.

They zealously studied the law, fanatically reflecting on its teaching. They read it, wrote it, recited it, memorized it, taught it, and preached it. Their work, to a fault, was mental work. Yet, Jesus does not throw out the baby with the bathwater. He instructs them to love the Lord with their heart, soul, and *mind*.

If the Pharisees raced to the mind while passing over the heart, twenty-first-century Christians tend toward the opposite. We tend to race to the heart, bypassing the mind. Yet, Jesus—and all of Scripture— calls us to glorify God with our minds as well as our hearts. However, due to our sin nature, obedience in this requires significant effort.

The Noetic Consequences of the Fall

Back in the garden of Eden, when Adam and Eve sinned, they plunged every aspect of humanity into sin. This fallen-ness includes our actions, our emotions, our wills, and our minds.

Theologians refer to the fallen-ness of our minds as, "the noetic consequence of the Fall" or "the noetic effects of sin." The word *noetic* comes from the Greek word *noētikos*, which means "intellectual" and refers to the mind or to the intellect. So, the phrase, "the noetic effects of sin," means that we do not naturally think, naturally meditate on, or naturally reason as we should.

This is not to say that our minds are absolutely ruined, incapable of analytical thought, constructive ideas, or spiritual thinking. Rather, it means that we are incapable of fulfilling our original, optimal capacity in this regard. As Craig and Moreland noted, "The Fall brought about the perversion of human faculties, but it did not destroy those faculties. Human reasoning and abilities are affected but not eliminated."[2]

A Renewed Mind

The good news is, when we become Christians, God redeems our minds like the rest of our personhood. It does not mean that through conversion we receive a higher I.Q., but it does mean that, for once, we can truly honor God with our minds.

At conversion, we receive "the mind of Christ" (1 Cor. 2:16). Like other dimensions of the Christian life, this is something God does in us, through the ministry of the Holy Spirit, but it is also something we are responsible to pursue and cultivate.

To this end, let's reflect more closely on two passages. First, writing to believers in Rome, the apostle Paul implores Christians, "do not be conformed to this age, but be transformed by the renewing of your mind, so that you may discern what is the good, pleasing, and perfect will of God" (Rom. 12:2).

Additionally, consider Paul's counsel to the believers in Colossae: "Set your mind on things above, not on earthly things. For you died, and your life is hidden with Christ in God. When Christ, who is your life, appears, then you will also appear with him in glory" (Col. 3:2–4).

In other words, Christians are to think Christianly. As Os Guinness argues, "Thinking Christianly is thinking by Christians about anything and everything in a consistently Christian way—in a manner that is shaped, directed, and restrained by the truth of God's Word and God's Spirit."[3]

How do we accomplish this? How does the gospel impact our minds? How do we cultivate a renewed mind, with thoughts, deliberations, and ideas that honor him? Let's consider renewing our minds in three different, yet mutually reinforcing, dimensions.

Filling Your Mind

The first step toward renewing your mind is the steady intake of God's Word. Peter calls Christians to "desire the pure milk of the word, so that you may grow up into your salvation" (1 Pet. 2:2).

This is an ongoing process for every believer throughout our Christian lives, but usually the early years after our conversion serve as an inflection point. That was certainly true in my case.

I became a believer in college. I was a political science major and a history minor. I aimed to attend law school, and then, perhaps, pursue a career in politics. I still enjoyed—and do enjoy—reading history and politics, but my appetite for God's Word became voracious, far outstripping history and political science texts.

I can still recall sitting in the back of "poly sci" classes, listening to my professor lecture on political theory, but my mind being in another place. I am not encouraging this pattern as a way of life; I am merely reflecting on my personal experiences.

I would hunch over, hiding myself behind the broad-shouldered young man seated in front of me, plop my pocket New Testament on my desk, and read away. What was going on? As a newborn babe in Christ, I was longing for the pure milk of the Word. I was reading God's Word, taking in the Scriptures.

Yet, we cannot be content to merely read the Bible; we must make sure to meditate on it. Historically, meditation was a distinctly Christian practice, but these days it rings in the ear like an Eastern religion. Unlike Eastern religions, Christian meditation is not about emptying the mind; it is about filling it.

The Puritans were masters at meditating on Scripture, and the Puritan era was, perhaps, the height of Christian meditation. The Puritans understood that Bible reading without application leads to spiritual imbalance and frustration. Consider Thomas Manton's reflection on Bible intake and mediation:

> The end of study is information, and the end of meditation is practice, or a work upon the affections. Study is like a winter sun that shines but does not warm, but meditation is like blowing up the fire, where we do not mind the blaze but the heat. The end of study is to hoard up truth, but of meditation to lay it forth in conference or holy

conversation. In study, we are rather like vintners that take in wine to store themselves for sale; in meditation, like those that buy wine for their own use and comfort. A vintner's cellar may be better stored than a nobleman's; the student may have more of notion and knowledge, but the practical Christian has more of taste and refreshment.[4]

Manton was right. When Bible reading leads to Bible meditation, something magical happens. The Word truly fills, shapes, and sanctifies our mind. That is why the Bible makes such profound promises regarding Scripture meditation. It promises knowledge of God's blessing and yields spiritual fruit in our lives (see Ps. 1; Josh. 1:5–9).

In fact, why don't you, right now, pause and meditate on God's promise in Joshua 1:8: "This book of instruction must not depart from your mouth; you are to meditate on it day and night so that you may carefully observe everything written in it. For then you will prosper and succeed in whatever you do."

Do you see how mediation works? Further clarity is given by David Mathis. He writes,

With meditation, we're not just storing up for transformation later, but enjoying food for our soul and experiencing transformation today. And when the focus is more on feeding and shaping, then constant review is less important.

Once-memorized, now-forgotten texts aren't a tragedy, but an opportunity to meditate and mold your mind even more.[5]

In addition to reading and meditating on Scripture, you can also receive it by sitting under sound preaching, listening to audio Bible readings, and, of course, memorizing it. Whatever the means, the first key is to fill your mind.

Guarding Your Mind

If filling your mind refers to what you take in, guarding your mind refers to what you keep out. This is a challenge. We live in an age of visual saturation, ever-present social media, and pursuing temptation.

Again, we tend to think of temptation as a matter of the heart, but it is just as much a matter of the mind. The information we let in, the thoughts we entertain, the ideas we foster, all can do much good—or much evil. Of course, there is pornography, which is destroying lives, marriages, and families at epidemic rates.

Consider these statistics related to pornography:

- Every second, 28,258 users are watching pornography on the Internet.
- Every second, $3,075.64 is being spent on pornography on the Internet.
- Every second, 372 people are typing the word *adult* into search engines.

- Forty million American people regularly visit porn sites.
- Thirty-five percent of all Internet downloads are related to pornography.
- Twenty-five percent of all search engine queries are related to pornography, or about 68 million search queries a day.[6]

Yet, as Christians, we have our marching orders. *We are* destroying speculations and every lofty thing raised up against the knowledge of God, and *we are* taking every thought captive to the obedience of Christ (see 2 Cor. 10:5).

We guard our minds not only by what we keep out, but by what we choose to dwell on. Our thought life is a powerful tool, for better or worse. What we determine to think on is, in many ways, determinative for our spiritual lives. That is why the apostle Paul exhorts us accordingly, "Finally, brothers and sisters, whatever is true, whatever is honorable, whatever is just, whatever is pure, whatever is lovely, whatever is commendable—if there is any moral excellence and if there is anything praiseworthy—dwell on these things" (Phil. 4:8).

In the spirit of the above text, John Bloom observed, *"The mind must be directed.* If we want to be happy, our trust must have its sights set on the right destination."[7]

Framing Your Mind

Lastly, not only are we to fill our minds and guard them, we are to frame them as well. By this I mean we are to cultivate, intentionally, a biblical outlook, or paradigm, through which we view and interpret the world. We can only do this through scriptural intake. The intake of the Word reframes our outlook and gives us a theological foundation to engage life and view the world, and to process all of life from a Christian worldview.

Michael Wittmer defines *worldview* as "a framework of fundamental concepts or beliefs about the world. In short, a worldview comprises the lens through which we see the world."[8]

Everyone has a worldview. Both believers and unbelievers function by a set of beliefs, presuppositions, and assumptions they make about life. Francis Schaeffer correctly stated,

> People function on the basis of their worldview more consistently than even they themselves may realize. The problem is not outward things. The problem is having, and then acting upon, the right worldview—the worldview which gives men and women the truth of what is.[9]

For Christians, essential to the process of renewing our minds is cultivating a biblical worldview. Thus, we train our minds to think biblically about grand, life-shaping realities and principles like creation, human existence, human relationships and sexuality, the afterlife, and every other touch point of intellectual formation.

In Conclusion

I began this chapter noting that Christianity is both a religion of the heart and the mind. This is true. Christians often err on both ends of the spectrum, most often on the heart end. But, we must understand that, ultimately, the renewing of the mind is to lead to a renewed person—affecting the totality of our personhood. In other words, the mind is to feed and shape the heart.

Prophetically, John Piper observes:

> If a person doesn't move from intellectual awareness of God and right thinking about God to an emotional embrace of God, he hasn't loved God with his mind. The mind has not yet loved until it hands off its thoughts to the emotions where they're embraced. And then the mind and the heart are working in what feels like such harmony, and you experience it as both intellectual and affectional love for God.[10]

May this be true of us, and may the gospel deeply affect our minds and our hearts for our own Christian growth and for the broader glory of God in our lives.

The Gospel &
Your Church

Have you ever heard someone say, "I am into Jesus, but not the church"? Or, put another way, "I am a Christian, but I do not believe in going to church"? Over my years as a pastor, I have encountered phrases like these many times. Let me share two stories, both from my first year as a pastor.

My first encounter with "Jesus, yes; church, no" theology came as a newly-minted pastor. My wife and I were hosting an open house in the church parsonage, where we lived. About half-a-dozen young families attended the gathering. All was going as planned until I began to talk about church membership. One gentleman in attendance pressed me on the topic, arguing the concept was unbiblical. I squirmed and tried to answer. Undaunted, he continued to press his case.

On another occasion, just a few months later, I was visiting a community member who had an infirmed child. The young girl's situation was dire, and the family requested I come over to pray with them. During my visit, I inquired about them spiritually. Confidently, they asserted they were believers in Jesus. When I asked them about their church membership, they said, "We are wanting to get back to being like the early-church Christians and have our own worship in our home."

Both conversations caught me off-guard, a bit flat-footed, and they forced me into an on-the-spot apologetic for the local church. For a moment, I felt uncertain of how to respond and embarrassed by my lack of clear answer.

Yet, what I intuitively knew then, and have come to understand more fully, is that Christianity is inextricably linked to the local church. In fact, the local church is the New Testament's expression of Christianity. The New Testament depicts the Christian and the local church together, like hand in glove. That's why I agree with Jonathan Parnell, who argues, "Membership in your local church is one of the most important things about you."[1]

Avoiding Extremes: Individualism and Institutionalism

As I serve the church now more broadly as a seminary president, I consistently bump into two unhealthy extremes—both of which misestimate the role of the church.

First, and most common in evangelical circles, is spiritual *individualism*.

This extreme so prioritizes a personal relationship with Christ that it forgets the role of the church. Conversion is a personal encounter with Christ and growth in Christ is fundamentally the same thing. One is nourished spiritually through books, conferences, podcasts, para-church ministries, and Bible studies.

The other extreme is an *institutional* approach to Christianity.

In its most unhealthy form, it is seen in traditional Roman Catholicism that holds "no salvation outside the church," and necessitates receiving the sacraments for salvation.

Yet, for evangelicals, some operate one tick away, especially denominations or individuals who are in closer proximity to the Roman Catholic Church. This institutional error equates salvation with church membership and Christian growth with church activity.

Both of these extremes miscommunicate the Christian life. Conversion is an individual experience that is intended to become a congregational reality. It is simply impossible to conceptualize New Testament Christianity apart from the local church.

Here is the point: when you were saved, you were saved into the church. When you were baptized, you were baptized into the church. When you believed the gospel, Jesus did not only rescue you; he transplanted you into the church.

The Church Universal, the Church Local

Another common misconception concerns the church universal and the church local. The church universal refers to all the redeemed, globally. The church universal also refers to the invisible church because we ultimately are not able to know who or how many comprise it.

Yet, most every reference in the New Testament is about the church local. By local church, I mean a group of Christians who are a part of a collective, covenant group, who meet together for worship and ministry.

As to membership, many today argue that the concept is not in the Bible. But the early church *did* keep a roll, at least in some form. We see the early church mentioning numbers of additions and baptisms and documenting terms for inclusion in—and exclusion from—the church. How could the New Testament authors report on these matters without some form of a membership roll?

The New Testament and the Church

More broadly, when you survey the New Testament you see it is all about the church. In Matthew 16, Jesus declared, "I will build my church, and the gates of Hades will not overpower it" (Matt. 16:18). Jesus fulfilled this promise through his own death, having shed his blood for the church (see Acts 20:28).

The book of Acts begins with the birth of the church through Peter's preaching at Pentecost. The story line of Acts is the church metastasizing, spreading throughout the Mediterranean region—and beyond—through the apostles' preaching.

The New Testament epistles were all written to or about churches. In them, the authors explain what churches are to believe and teach, and how they are to minister and organize themselves. At the end of the New Testament—the book of Revelation—the apostle John records Jesus' seven letters to seven churches and punctuates the Bible's conclusion with Jesus' dramatic return for his bride, the church.

In fact, Jesus likens the church to himself. Remember the scene we saw earlier in this book from Acts 9 when Jesus confronted Saul on the Damascus Road? He asked, "Saul, Saul, why are you persecuting me?" (v. 4).

Effectively, Jesus equated the church with himself; how one views, engages, and treats the church reflects how one views, engages, and treats Jesus.

The New Testament makes following Christ and local church participation essentially synonymous. That is why, as John Piper has observed, "In the New Testament, to be excluded from the local church was to be excluded from Christ."[2]

New Testament Pictures of the Church

Importantly, the New Testament depicts the church in multiple ways, each reflecting the corporate, collective nature of the church—and of Christians who are a part of it. Consider three word pictures referencing the church: body, building, and flock. Let's reflect on passages pertaining to each.

The Body

- "Now you are the body of Christ, and individual members of it" (1 Cor. 12:27).
- "Now as we have many parts in one body, and all the parts do not have the same function, in the same way we who are many are one body in Christ and individually members of one another" (Rom. 12:4–5).
- "So that there would be no division in the body, but that the members would have the same

concern for each another. So if one member suf-
fers, all the members suffer with it; if one member is honored, all the members rejoice with it"
(1 Cor. 12:25–26).

- "Let the peace of Christ, to which you were also
  called in one body, rule in your hearts. And be
  thankful" (Col. 3:15).

The Flock

- "Jesus said again, 'Truly I tell you, I am the gate
  for the sheep. . . . I am the gate. If anyone enters
  by me, he will be saved and will come in and go
  out and find pasture'" (John 10:7, 9).
- "'I am the good shepherd. The good shepherd
  lays down his life for the sheep'" (John 10:11).
- "I exhort the elders among you as a fellow elder
  and witness to the sufferings of Christ, as well
  as one who shares in the glory about to be
  revealed: Shepherd God's flock among you, not
  overseeing out of compulsion but willingly, as
  God would have you; not out of greed for money
  but eagerly; not lording it over those entrusted to
  you, but being examples to the flock. And when
  the chief Shepherd appears, you will receive the
  unfading crown of glory" (1 Pet. 5:1–4).

The Building

- "So then you are no longer foreigners and strangers, but fellow citizens with the saints, and members of God's household, built on the foundation of the apostles and prophets, with Christ Jesus himself as the cornerstone. In him the whole building, being put together, grows into a holy temple in the Lord. In him you are also being built together for God's dwelling in the Spirit" (Eph. 2:19–22).

The Sum Is Greater than Its Parts

The staggering biblical truth is that when the church comes together, the sum total is greater than its parts. Jonathan Parnell rightly observed, "The local church is the greatest, most profound collective of which any human could be a part. Your family, your career, your nationality—these all pale in comparison to what it means to be a member of a local church.[3]"

How is the sum greater than its parts? In three distinct ways. And herein we see both why and how the gospel connects your life to the church. Together you enjoy collective worship, collective ministry, and collective witness.

Collective Worship

As we again review the New Testament, we see the church gathering was standard operating procedure. Regularly, they gathered in homes to sit under the teaching of the Word and to break bread together. As the church developed, we see the primacy of the Lord's Day and the practice of gathering for worship on the first day of the week—the day of Christ's resurrection.

Those who neglected gathering with God's people received a stern warning. The author of Hebrews warned believers of "not neglecting to gather together, as some are in the habit of doing, but encouraging each another, and all the more as you see the day approaching" (Heb. 10:25).

Believers today would be wise to heed this sage advice and to join a church body for all the benefits of collective worship, as well as encouraging others—who might argue otherwise—to do the same.

Collective Ministry

When you became a believer, God granted you spiritual gifting for the betterment of the local church. Reflect on the following passages:

- "And he himself gave some to be apostles, some prophets, some evangelists, some pastors and teachers, equipping the saints for the work of ministry, to build up the body of Christ, until we all reach unity in the faith and in the knowledge of God's Son, growing into maturity with a stature measured by Christ's fullness" (Eph. 4:11–13).

- "According to the grace given to us, we have different gifts: If prophecy, use it according to the proportion of one's faith; if service, use it in service; if teaching, in teaching; if exhorting, in exhortation; giving, with generosity; leading, with diligence; showing mercy, with cheerfulness" (Rom. 12:6–8).

David Mathis rightly notes, "Living the Christian life in community is more than just loose associations, but committing to each other to be there for each other when life is hard, in sickness and in sorrow."[4]

Along the same line, Richard Baxter helpfully states,

We have greater work here to do than merely securing our own salvation. We are members of the world and church, and we must labor to do good to many. We are trusted with our Master's talents for his service, in our places to do our best to propagate his truth, and grace, and church; and to bring home souls, and honor his cause, and edify his flock, and further the salvation of as many as we can. All this is to be done on earth, if we will secure the end of all in heaven.[5]

So, let me encourage you to dust off your spiritual giftings and employ them with great joy to edify your fellow believers within the local church context, and to reach the lost for Christ.

Collective Witness

A lone-ranger Christian doesn't make the best witness for Christ. Rather, someone who is grounded, has a home, and is part of a solid covenant community of support is best prepared to draw others into the kingdom.[6]

The local church is a community of Christians who live as the on-the-ground expression of the supremacy of Jesus by advancing his gospel in distance and depth.[7]

The great British preacher C. H. Spurgeon said, "If I had never joined a church till I had found one that was perfect, I should never have joined one at all; and the moment I did join it, if I had found one, I should have spoiled it, for it would not have been a perfect church after I had become a member of it. Still, imperfect as it is, it is the dearest place on earth to us."[8]

It is vital to understand that there is no perfect church. That is because the church is comprised of sinners—redeemed sinners. So, do not be a perennial church shopper. As my seminary professor, Chip Stam, often reminded the class, "The maturing believer is easily edified."

God uses each of his children's gifts in a unique way to fulfill the mission he has for the church as a whole. Make sure that you're upholding your end of the bargain.

In Conclusion

Popular Christian musician Tripp Lee is right: "There is no good, healthy, regular pattern of the Christian life if you are not joined with a local church—if you are not in covenant with other Christians."[9]

Ultimately, Jesus has redeemed you to be a creature in community—a Christian living out the gospel in consent with other Christians, the church.

CONCLUSION

The Gospel & You

After his resurrection and just before his ascension, Jesus delivered a final charge to his disciples. We refer to it as the Great Commission. Recorded at the end of all four Gospels and at the beginning of the book of Acts, the Great Commission is the church's permanent marching orders. It's Jesus' abiding expectation of every believer, in every place, in every era. Jesus instructs us in Matthew 28:18–20:

> "All authority has been given to me in heaven and on earth. Go, therefore, and make disciples of all nations, baptizing them in the name of the Father and of the Son and of the Holy Spirit, teaching them to observe everything I commanded you. And remember, I am with you always, to the end of the age."

Every healthy church rightly prioritizes the Great Commission, as does every healthy Christian. Further, churches are called to fulfill the Great Commission in a multitude of ways, as are individual Christians.

For many of us, living the Christian life and influencing others for Christ have largely been event driven. Faithful Christian living best evidences itself through faithfully attending church activities. Faithful Christian witness entails participating in the church's periodic outreach events. But as we've seen throughout this book, the Christian life isn't an event; it's a way of life. Conveying the gospel isn't merely a conversation; it's also a lifestyle. When you became a Christian, you didn't join a club; you were birthed into a new family. Now, for us, life is lived in every way in, by, and with the gospel of Christ.

A Great Change

For me, this all began to come into focus during my college years. As I referenced at the beginning of this book, I came to know Christ while a college athlete. Though reared in a Christian home, I didn't surrender my life to Christ until I was eighteen.

I still recall the early days of my new life in Christ. I was like the blind man healed by Jesus in John 9. At that point, I had no seminary degree, and I knew very little about what it meant to be a Christian. But I did know that Jesus had changed my life. He had forgiven me, saved me, and made me a new person in him. And I was eager to share that life change with others.

The ramifications of my new birth continue to work themselves out in my life. The more I grow in Christ, the more I understand all that change included—namely, it is to impact every dimension of my life. More than a ministry category or a Sunday category or a family category, it is to impact every area of my life.

A Great Opportunity

As the gospel impacts every area of my life, my witness is infinitely more consistent and more robust, and when I am most satisfied in Christ, then I most faithfully represent him.

This life change is meant to be external, radiating out from us to others. Francis of Assisi is attributed with the famous saying, "Preach the gospel and use words if necessary." The saying is off target (we must use words to share the gospel!), but the sentiment is not. Our lives are to be a constant fragrance of Christ, naturally reflecting his life. Our words must be, and can be, backed up by our lives. As those two are in alignment, we become a potent gospel witness.

It's Christ's Power, Not Ours

Finally, I want to remind you it is Christ's power, not ours, that enables this to occur. To illustrate this, I want to borrow a story from the great preacher, A. J. Gordon.

A Christian leader of the nineteenth century, Gordon was a prolific hymn writer, preacher, and educator, having helped found the Gordon Bible Institute and having served as its first president.

Gordon once told the story of attending the World's Fair in Chicago. While there, he saw, from a distance, a gentleman working a hand-pump well. Perhaps you've seen one of these before on an old farm. Recall how they work: you grip the lever and vigorously work the pump up and down, drawing water up from the underground well. That's what Gordon saw the man doing.

Gordon, however, was intrigued at how aggressively the man was working the well; he was nonstop, frenetically pumping it up and down. Curious, Gordon decided to take a closer look. As he drew nearer, he noticed a funny thing. The man wasn't working the well; the well was working the man.

Evidently, the pump sat atop an artesian well, where the water-flow naturally gushed upward. As a joke, someone had attached a wooden cutout of a man, hinged elbow and all, and attached it to the well.

Thus, from a distance, everyone was impressed at how aggressively and indefatigably the man was working the well, but upon a closer view, all could see the well was working the man. In that moment, Gordon saw an analogy for the Christian life—and so do I.

In the Christian life, pumping the well leads to a dry, lifeless, works-oriented Christianity. And if we are not careful, it can grow into legalism and hypocrisy. But when the Word and Spirit dwell richly within us, the gospel truly percolates throughout our lives, the church life moves from duty to delight, and the trust of the Spirit ripens and abounds. This is what I want for my life. This is what I want for yours.

This book has been about how the Christian life—that which is lived fully in Christ—extends into every area of our existence. Further, it is about how, as we intentionally let his life permeate ours, every aspect of our lives becomes a potent gospel witness.

Intentionality

So, dear friend, here is where we conclude this book. The secret to the Christian life is: there's really no secret. It is simply loving, and intentionally living, for Jesus. We apply the gospel to every area of our lives. We bring the Scripture to bear on every aspect of our lives. We submit every area of our lives to Christ and his lordship. As we do, the life of Christ pulsates through us. We live a more joy-filled, satisfied life. As we reflect through every aspect of our lives, we experience the joy and wholeness that only Christ can give. I pray you experience this joy and wholeness.

Acknowledgments

Like any book project, this one could not have come to completion without God's grace to me through the support of family, friends, and colleagues.

At the personal level, my life and ministry is enabled and enriched by the prayers and encouragement of my family. God has abundantly blessed me with a wife in Karen, and children in Anne-Marie, Caroline, William, Alden, and Elizabeth, who have surpassed my every hope and dream as to what they'd be and mean to me. They are a constant source of love, joy, and support. To my favorite six people on the planet, thank you.

At the institutional level, my colleagues and office staff likewise are an invaluable source of support and encouragement. Most especially, I'm thankful for Patrick Hudson, Tyler Sykora, Dawn Philbrick, and Catherine Crouse. These men and women are an absolute delight to serve with, and they go about their daily tasks with graciousness and competence. Thank you.

Furthermore, I'm thankful to the team at B&H Publishing Group, most especially Jennifer Lyell, Devin Maddox, and Taylor Combs. Thank you, dear friends, for believing in this project and for working with me to bring it to fruition.

Last, and most of all, I'm indebted to my Lord and Savior, Jesus Christ. Like every other ministerial undertaking, none of this would be possible without his grace, calling, and enabling. May this book, and all that I do, bring him much glory.

About the Author

Elected on October 15, 2012, Dr. Jason K. Allen serves as the fifth president of Midwestern Baptist Theological Seminary, in Kansas City, Missouri, and is one of the youngest presidents in all of American higher education.

Since coming to Midwestern Seminary, he has led the institution to become one of the largest and fastest growing seminaries in North America. In addition to his role as president, Dr. Allen serves the institution in the classroom, as an associate professor for preaching and pastoral ministry.

More broadly, he serves the church through his preaching and writing ministries as well. He is the author of two recently-released books, *The SBC & the 21st Century* (B&H Publishing) and *Discerning Your Call to Ministry* (Moody Publishing). Dr. Allen regularly posts essays on his website, jasonkallen.com, and hosts a weekly podcast, "Preaching & Preachers," which can also be found at jasonkallen.com.

Before coming to Midwestern Seminary, Dr. Allen served as a pastor, and as a senior administrator at The Southern Baptist Theological Seminary in Louisville, Kentucky. He and his wife, Karen, are both from Mobile, Alabama, and have five children: Anne-Marie, Caroline, William, Alden, and Elizabeth.

NOTES

Chapter 2

1. John R. W. Stott, *The Cross of Christ* (Downers Grove, IL: InterVarsity Press, 1986), 234.

2. John Flavel, *The Mystery of Providence* (London: L. B. Seeley and Song, 1824; repr., Apollo, PA: Ichthus Publications, 2014), 67.

3. Phillip Holmes, from his article, "What Is Your Biggest Regret?" as found at http://www.desiringgod.org/articles /what-is-your-biggest-regret.

4. Ralph F. Wilson, from his article, "Amazing Grace, the Story of John Newton, Author of America's Favorite Hymn," as found at http:www.joyfulheart.com/misc/newton.htm.

Chapter 3

1. Wayne Grudem, "Personal Reflections on the History of CBMW and the State of the Gender Debate," *Journal for Biblical Manhood & Womanhood* (2009), accessed Feb. 22, 2017 from http://cbmw.org/uncategorized/personal-reflections -on-the-history-of-CBMW-and-the-state-of-the-gender -debate.

Chapter 4

1. This statistic was accessed at http://www.apa.org /topics/divorce/.

2. This statistic was accessed at http://www.cdc.gov /nchs/nvss/marriage_divorce_tables.htm.

3. This statistic was accessed at https://www.mckinley irvin.com/Family-Law-Blog/2012/October/32-Shocking -Divorce-Statistics.aspx.

4. This statistic was accessed at https://www.barna.com /research/majority-of-americans-now-believe-in-cohabitation/.

5. Charles Spurgeon, "A Pastoral Visit," *Metropolitan Tabernacle Pulpit*, vol. 54 (London: Passmore and Alabaster, 1908; repr., Pasadena, TX: Pilgrim, 1978), 363.

6. David Mathis, from his article, "Ask Your Child to Forgive You," as found at http://www.desiringgod.org /articles/ask-your-child-to-forgive-you.

Chapter 5

1. David Mathis, in his article, "Manage Your Time for the Mission of Love," as found at http://www.desiringgod.org /articles/manage-your-time-for-the-mission-of-love.

2. Donald S. Whitney, *Spiritual Disciplines for the Christian Life*, revised and updated. ed. (Colorado Springs, CO: NavPress, 2014), 137–38.

3. Jonathan Edwards [1716], *Letters and Personal Writings* (WJE Online Vol. 16), ed. George S. Claghorn, as found at http://edwards.yale.edu/archive?path=aHR0cDovL2Vkd2FyZ HMueWFsZS5lZHUvY2dpLWJpbi9uZXRdwaGlsby9nZXRvYmpl Y3QucGw/Yy4xNTo3NDoxLndqZW8=.

4. C. T. Studd, from the poem, "Only One Life Twill Soon Be Past," as found at http://paulhockley.com/2016/05/24 /quote-only-one-life-twill-soon-be-past-poem-by-c-t-studd/.

Chapter 6

1. John Piper, in his article, "Free from Money, Rich Toward God," as found at http://www.desiringgod.org /messages/free-from-money-rich-toward-god.

2. Harold Myra and Marshall Shelley, *The Leadership Secrets of Billy Graham* (Grand Rapids, MI: Zondervan, 2005), 118.

3. Paul David Tripp, in his article, "Do I Love Money: One Simple Test," as found at http://www.desiringgod.org /interviews/do-i-love-money-one-simple-test.

4. Ray Ortlund, in his article, "Greater Wealth," as found at https://blogs.thegospelcoalition.org/rayortlund/2014/12/02 /greater-wealth/.

Chapter 7

1. James M. Hamilton Jr., *Work and Our Labor in the Lord* (Wheaton, IL: Crossway, 2017), 91.

2. Leland Ryken, *Redeeming the Time: A Christian Approach to Work and Leisure* (Grand Rapids, MI: Baker Books, 1995), 184.

3. Gene Edward Veith, *God at Work: Your Christian Vocation in All of Life* (Wheaton, IL: Crossway Books, 2011), 14–15.

4. Keith Welton, in his article, "Six Ways God's at Work in You—at Work," as found at http://www.desiringgod.org /articles/six-ways-god-s-at-work-in-you-at-work.

5. Marshall Segal, in his article, "100,000 Hours: Eight Aims for Your Career," as found at http://www.desiringgod .org/articles/100-000-hours-eight-aims-for-your-career.

6. John Piper quoted in Hamilton Jr., *Work and Our Labor in the Lord*, 23.

7. Timothy Keller and Katherine Leary Alsdorf, *Every Good Endeavor: Connecting Your Work to God's Work* (New York, NY: Riverhead Books, 2012), 149.

Chapter 8

1. Paul Heintzman, *Leisure and Spirituality: Biblical, Historical, and Contemporary Perspectives* (Grand Rapids, MI: Baker Academic, 2015), found at http://www.desiringgod. org/articles/rethinking-our-relaxing.

2. John Piper, in his article, "Softball, Sex, and Augustus Strong," as found at http://www.desiringgod.org/articles /softball-sex-and-augustus-strong.

3. As found in Donald S. Whitney, *Spiritual Disciplines for the Christian Life* (Colorado Springs, CO: NavPress, 1997), 95.

4. Joe Thorn, in his article, "Two Keys to Better Recreation," as found at http://ftc.co/resource-library /blog-entries/two-keys-to-better-recreation.

5. Timothy George, *Reading Scripture with the Reformers* (Downers Grove, IL: InterVarsity Press Academic, 2011), 20.

Chapter 9

1. Augustine, *Confessions* (Tustin: Xist Publishing, 2015), 1.

2. James Porter Moreland and William Lane Craig, *Philosophy of Science: Philosophical Foundations for a Christian Worldview* (Seoul: Christian Literature Crusade, 2013), 18.

3. Quoted in James Emery White, *Mind for God* (Downers Grove, IL: InterVarsity Press, 2013), 20–21.

4. *The Christian Observer, Conducted by Members of the Established Church . . . From the London Edition* (Boston, MA: W. Wells, 1818), 696.

5. David Mathis, in his article, "Memorize the Mind of God," as found at http://www.desiringgod.org/articles/memorize -the-mind-of-god.

6. Statistics from the article, "Internet Pornography by the Numbers" as found at https://www.webroot.com/us/en/home /resources/tips/digital-family-life/internet-pornography-by -the-numbers.

7. John Bloom, in his article, "How to Get Your Mind Back on Track," found at http://www.desiringgod.org/articles /how-to-get-your-mind-back-on-track.

8. Michael Eugene Wittmer, *Heaven Is a Place on Earth: Why Everything You Do Matters to God* (Grand Rapids, MI: Zondervan, 2004), 21.

9. Francis A. Schaeffer, *The Complete Works of Francis A. Schaeffer: A Christian Worldview,* vol. 5, *A Christian View of the West* (Wheaton, IL: Crossway Books, 1985), 252.

10. John Piper, in his article, "What Does It Mean to Love the Lord with All Your Mind?" as found at http:// www.desiringgod.org/interviews/what-does-it-mean-to-love -the-lord-with-all-your-mind.

Chapter 10

1. Jonathan Parnell, in his article, "The Local Church and the Supremacy of Christ," as found at http://www.desiringgod. org/articles/the-local-church-and-the-supremacy-of-christ.

2. John Piper, in his article, "How Important Is Church Membership," found at http://www.desiringgod.org/messages /how-important-is-church-membership.

3. Parnell, "The Local Church and the Supremacy of Christ."

4. David Mathis, in his article, "Why Join a Church," found at http://www.desiringgod.org/articles/why-join-a-church.

5. Richard Baxter and Leonard Bacon, *Select Practical Writings of Richard Baxter, with a Life of the Author* (New Haven: Durrie & Peck, 1831), 153.

6. Mathis, "Why Join a Church."

7. Ibid.

8. C. H. Spurgeon and Tom Carter, *Spurgeon at His Best: Over 2200 Striking Quotations from the World's Most Exhaustive and Widely-Read Sermon Series* (Grand Rapids, MI: Baker, 1988).

9. Tripp Lee, in his article, "You Need the Local Church to Be Healthy," found at http://www.desiringgod.org/articles/you-need-the-local-church-to-be-healthy.